HARVEY INGHAM and GARDNER COWLES, SR.

Things Don't Just Happen

HARVEY INGHAM AND
Things Don't

THE IOWA STATE UNIVERSITY

GARDNER COWLES, SR.
Just Happen

By GEORGE MILLS

Edited by JOAN BUNKE

PRESS / AMES, IOWA / 1 9 7 7

GEORGE S. MILLS joined the staff of *The Marshalltown Times-Republican* in 1928 after receiving a degree in journalism from Northwestern University. Subsequently, he worked as a reporter and editor for the Iowa Daily Press Association, the Associated Press and *The Cedar Rapids Gazette*. From 1943 to 1971, he was legislative reporter and political writer for *The Des Moines Register* and in 1976 he became legislative reporter for Des Moines' WHO-TV. He won the Iowa Associated Press annual news writing sweepstakes award three times. His book *Rogues and Heroes From Iowa's Amazing Past* is based upon two of the numerous historical series and articles he has written, "In Old Des Moines" and "Iowa's Amazing Past." He also is author of *The Little Man With the Long Shadow*, a biography of Des Moines pioneer Frederick M. Hubbell.

JOAN BUNKE, a 1955 graduate of the University of Wisconsin School of Journalism, has worked on the editorial staffs of *The Des Moines Register* and *The Des Moines Tribune* since 1959 as an editor, critic and reporter.

© 1977 The Des Moines Register and Tribune Company
Ames, Iowa 50010. All rights reserved

Composed by The Des Moines Register and Tribune Company
Printed by The Iowa State University Press

First edition, 1977

Library of Congress Cataloging in Publication Data

Mills, George S
    Harvey Ingham and Gardner Cowles, Sr.: Things don't just happen.

    1. Des Moines Register and Tribune Company. 2. Ingham, Harvey, 1858–1949. 3. Cowles, Gardner, 1861–1946. 4. Journalists—Iowa—Biography. I. Title.
PN4899.D485R45   071′.77′58   77–23393
ISBN 0–8138–0155–9

CONTENTS

ACKNOWLEDGMENTS

The author acknowledges with appreciation the aid of the many individuals he interviewed and corresponded with to gather material for this book.

Sources consulted included many editions of a number of Iowa newspapers, among them *The Iowa Star, Fort Des Moines Gazette, The Iowa Citizen, The Iowa State Register, The Des Moines Leader, The Des Moines Register and Leader, The Des Moines Register, The Des Moines Tribune, The Des Moines News, The Des Moines Capital, The Algona Upper Des Moines, The Algona Advance* as well as Webster City and Sioux City newspapers.

Other publications consulted included the *Annals* of Polk County and Des Moines, Johnson Brigham's *History of Des Moines and Polk County*, John L. Shover's *Cornbelt Rebellion: The Farmers' Holiday Association, Annals of Iowa, The Palimpsest* and *The Iowa Journal of History and Politics*.

I want also to extend my thanks to Robert Doyle for searching out clippings at *The Des Moines Register* and *Tribune* and Jon Robison for unearthing a large number of newspaper volumes for my use at the state historical department.

INTRODUCTION

The story told is 70 years old, but it sets up modern-day echoes of the style and spirit of *The Des Moines Register* of the 1970s. Today's *Register* is more sophisticated but as determined to publish a readable, competitive "quality product" as in its earlier, wobbly days. The story:

A worker tosses the last bundle of papers into the newspaper truck and shouts to the driver: "Step on it! You've got a minute and a half to catch the 11:40!" The truck roars out of the *Register* plant into dark streets. As the driver nears the Rock Island Railroad station, he sees the train start to move. He has missed the 11:40. That means that readers in several Iowa towns may not get their newspapers tomorrow morning. Making a swift decision, the driver swerves around a corner and speeds to a nearby street that crosses the railroad tracks. He parks the truck across the tracks, blocking the still slowly moving train. The train stops. Engineer and conductor shout predictable remarks. The driver makes his pitch: Take these papers and I'll get out of your way! When the train rolls again, the papers are in the baggage car.

The story probably is apocryphal, but it demonstrates the primary characteristics of the Cowles-Ingham era of Iowa newspapering, the era that administered emergency "rescue" treatment to a declining *Register* and turned it into a working economic and journalistic unit that became the direct ancestor of today's Register and Tribune Company newspapers, the morning *Des Moines Register*, the afternoon *Des Moines Tribune* and *The Des Moines Sunday Register*.

One hallmark of that early *Register* was the competitive spirit of staff members. A second was their concentration on getting the paper to the reader.

The driver's job did not require him to take extreme measures, yet getting the papers aboard that train was a serious matter to him personally.

He was part of the sense of pride that permeated the entire organization — news, advertising, circulation and mechanical departments. Such plant-wide enthusiasm was a major factor in the Cowles-Ingham papers' winning their fight for survival over competing Des Moines papers and in extending *Register* circulation over the entire state, of becoming a newspaper giant, a responsible giant.

Today, the *Sunday Register* and the daily *Register* and the daily *Tribune* are read in six of 10 Iowa homes. This is the story of the two men — Publisher Gardner Cowles, sr., and Editor Harvey Ingham — whose policies over the first 40 years of the Twentieth Century built the modern *Register* and *Tribune* organization.

It is, primarily, the story of a quest for quality. *The Register,* whose logotype slogan is "The Newspaper Iowa Depends Upon," is the only daily newspaper of general circulation across Iowa. One longtime editor summed up the tasks of *The Register* and its sister paper, *The Tribune*, in a company meeting: "Our job really begins where competing papers' jobs end, because our responsibility is to report on not just Iowa's individual communities but the state as a whole."

By "quality," that same editor said, "we mean competence and integrity. We mean a large staff with the talent, the skill, the professional training to find out and analyze what is happening in this state and with the integrity to report it honestly and forthrightly even if we momentarily lose a few friends in doing so."

This is the story of the two men who began that quest for quality.

HARVEY INGHAM and GARDNER COWLES, SR.

Things Don't Just Happen

1 ALGONA BEGINNINGS

They were two "small-town boys" from the northern Iowa community of Algona who early moved among the town's leading lights. Later, they became involved in politics — Republican, because that was the only kind that had any heft in the Iowa of the 1880s, the 1890s and the early years of the Twentieth Century.

Each had made his mark by early middle age, Gardner Cowles a country banker and investor of considerable prosperity, Harvey Ingham a country editor with an influential voice despite his small-town base.

However satisfying their Algona achievements, both decided at one of those critical watersheds in life — in their forties — to confront the challenge of trying to be big frogs in a bigger pond than Algona. Both had a fairly clear idea that the bigger pond, Des Moines, contained a considerable number of underwater obstacles, but both were optimistic of clearing them away.

They were longtime acquaintances, but they had been "enemies" of a sort. Through contention, they had taken the measure of each other.

They were products of the Nineteenth Century American frontier at its best, out of a background of upward-strivers who took advantage of every educational opportunity, honed their business talents and believed in trying to develop the best in others as well as in themselves. Believing in and living the Protestant work ethic, they practiced an individualism that let other individuals grow — an attitude with a "liberal" cast that colored their newspaper lives through subsequent decades.

Gardner Cowles was a perfectionist, early, late and always. This quality drove everyone who had dealings with him — his employees and his children alike — to distraction. Report a newspaper circulation peak, expecting praise, and he would ask you when you were going to reach the next goal. Come home with a high school report card, the way eldest son Russell Cowles used to, and Cowles would ask you not about the four *A*s but why you got the one *B*.

Cowles became a financial and political conservative, a businessman who knew how to get a firm into black ink and keep it there, and a cool personality whom one of his reporters eventually came to describe as "modest and retiring, but he could look right through you with his pale blue eyes and cut you on the other side." Paradoxically, Cowles teamed up with warm, "liberal" Editor Ingham to produce a study in contrasts and a newspaper that reflected both personalities.

The Ingham contrast was extreme; his jovial, booming voice, his geniality and his generosity earned him later in life the nickname "Uncle Harvey" as he distributed largesse to down-and-outers on his walk to his Des Moines office each morning. His charity made him so widely known that by 1936 the crowd waiting for his morning street-giving had grown out of hand. He finally had to call the paupers together, make "cash settlements" with each and stop the handouts.

In Des Moines, Ingham became one of the earliest editors to move toward making a newspaper geared to providing readers with unbiased reporting and confining editorial opinion to the editorial pages. Nationally, Ingham became respected for his leadership in human affairs, for his vision and courage and for his contributions to the growth and acceptance of *The Register* and its sister paper, *The Tribune*.

Despite the fact that they were anything but the Bobbsey twins of Iowa journalism, they came out of the same severe pioneer Iowa background; their fathers were mavericks — jousting with "popular opinion" and willing to take the consequences of unpopularity.

The personal contrasts and the two young men's different goals in Algona had led to a confrontation two decades before they became partners in Des Moines. In 1883, Ingham was asserting a strong editorial voice in his Algona paper, *The Upper Des Moines*. One of his targets was Cowles, who at the ripe age of 22 was Algona school superintendent. In five thundering editorials, Ingham attacked Cowles for buying a half-interest in *The Algona Repub-*

lican, a competitor of Ingham's *Upper Des Moines.*

"Fire him," Ingham wrote, blasting away at the "impropriety" of a school official's getting into the newspaper business. Besides, Ingham insisted, Cowles's "school work will necessarily suffer." On top of that, Ingham wrote, Cowles was "unfit" for the school post; someone new should be appointed, someone "old enough not to be attracted by side speculations and smart enough to only try to do one thing at a time."

The attacks did not budge Cowles, who continued as co-owner of the paper for more than a year afterward. Decades later, when Publisher Cowles and his editor, Ingham, had built *The Register* into a thriving success, Cowles could still quote in detail from the stinging comments Ingham made in 1883. Their friendship did not suffer any long-term damage from the quarrel, but the battle was bitter while it lasted because each man fought tenaciously for any cause he believed in.

They were crusty, independent-minded individuals who grew out of morally demanding Iowa pioneer families — high-principled and oriented toward high-minded goals — "achiever" families of the Nineteenth Century. Gardner Cowles's father was the personification of that century's father figure.

Spare, six feet tall, wearing a gray beard that reached to his waist, the Rev. William Fletcher Cowles ruled his God-fearing Methodist household with an iron hand and his listeners at pioneer revival meetings with a voice that boomed through the woods denouncing the devil and slavery in pre-Civil War Iowa. Born in New York State in 1819, he moved to Burlington, Iowa, in 1851 from Hannibal, Missouri, where he had been serving a church.

Gardner Cowles was born into the pioneer household in Oskaloosa, in south Iowa, Feb. 28, 1861. Less than two months later, on Apr. 13, Ft. Sumter, S. C., fell and the Civil War began. Repercussions of the bloody hostilities rolled through Gardner's early life, as deep an influence as the exacting religious fervor of his father and the fact that his 35-year-old mother, Marie, died when he was 12 years old and his brother LaMonte was 14. When she married William Cowles in 1857, he was a widower with three children; after her death, minister Cowles married a third time. For Gardner, it was an unfortunate marriage; "I never liked my stepmother," he said.

As presiding elder (district superintendent) of the

Methodist Church in the Oskaloosa region, William Cowles had battled fiercely for freedom for the black man in the pre-war era, even though many of his neighbors favored the institution of slavery. Some of them, in fact, violently supported slave-holding.

"Fearless as a lion," William Cowles faced at least one incident of mob action that threatened his safety, but he remained undisturbed by it. "He was as a flaming sword, passing around his district, emphasizing the gospel of freedom and insisting with Abraham Lincoln that no government could be perpetually half-slave and half-free," one of his associates said. Although many of his Methodist brethren did not follow his lead, Cowles supported Lincoln for president in 1860, when the Republican candidate carried the Cowleses' home county, Mahaska, winning 1,640 votes to Democrat Stephen A. Douglas's 1,331, and carrying Iowa 70,000 to 56,000. Later, William Cowles was to serve two terms as an Iowa district collector of U.S. revenue under a Lincoln appointment.

Like the fanatical slavery foe John Brown, who had passed through Des Moines a few times before the war escorting fugitive slaves, the Rev. Mr. Cowles felt he had been called by the Lord to preach the equality of man. On one occasion, in a sermon entitled "Political Filthiness," he expounded to a large Oskaloosa congregation on slavery. Said one observer: "Most of the brethren stood it bravely, but when Mr. Cowles married Moses to a black woman and declared that she was a full-blooded African, one fellow could stand it no longer. . . . He arose and hustled his way through the door."

In some churches, angry members refused to pay preachers who spoke against slavery. William Cowles called for donations for one such beleaguered preacher and the appeal produced two wagonloads of provisions.

Loneliness colored Gardner's childhood, at least partly because Methodist ministers were transferred frequently. The Cowles family moved every year or two, living in various Iowa towns, among them Mount Pleasant, Muscatine, Oskaloosa, Ottumwa, Grinnell, Eddyville, Knoxville and Albia. Friends young Gardner made in each town, friends not made easily for him, had to be left behind.

At home, the family met twice daily for prayers, and parents and children regularly consulted the Bible for advice and comfort. The family operated on a budget of $1 per person per week for all necessities, including food and clothing. Gardner later recalled that "at an early age, I knew that I would never have any money given to me, that I would never be helped to get jobs."

William F. Cowles never had much money of his own; he had saved some cash before coming to Iowa but "lost every cent he had in a Keokuk land boom." After that, he avoided speculation, never went into debt and died at age 80 in 1899 leaving no bills for his estate to pay. With that heritage, Gardner Cowles grew up a financial conservative who advised young people: "Never spend your last dollar." At home, idleness was akin to sin. More, the Rev. Mr. Cowles distrusted the temptations of town life, so he required his sons to work on farms in the summertime.

Young Gardner always had a job of some sort, from pasting strips of paper to hold buttons on their cards in a dry goods store to folding newspapers in the daily *Journal* office in Muscatine.

The rigor of his early years turned Gardner Cowles into a self-reliant individual who heeded home examples of honesty, integrity, thrift and hard work, and who had a pronounced zeal for self-improvement. Moving about with the family, he soaked up knowledge about Iowa cities, towns and counties, a background that was to be important to him as a newspaper publisher. He attended three Iowa colleges, spending his first year at William Penn College at Oskaloosa, the next two at Grinnell College and his fourth undergraduate year at Iowa Wesleyan College at Mount Pleasant, with mathematics as his favorite subject. He took his undergraduate bachelor of arts degree at Wesleyan in 1882, when he was 21. Three years later, he received a master of arts degree at Wesleyan.

As an Iowa Wesleyan student, Cowles continued his habit of making his own financial way, organizing a dinner club of 15 members to help hold down his own and others' expenses. He joined a fraternity, Phi Delta Theta, despite his frugalities, which included going a whole year wearing the same suit.

From his summer work on farms and from living in a number of farm towns, young Cowles picked up more information, adding to that store when, as a college student, he traveled on vacations from farm to farm selling maps of the United States and trading religious tracts for food and lodging with farmers. Decades later, when he sent agents out into the countryside selling newspaper subscriptions, his knowledge helped pave their way to success.

During one vacation, he worked on a survey crew setting up the rail route from Newburg, Iowa, north to State Center, and between his junior and senior college years he earned the large income of $75 a month plus room and board on a Union Pacific Railroad project in Wyoming and Idaho.

Cowles loved railroading and might have followed it as an occupation had he been able to find a lead to a promising job after graduation. What turned up was a short stint of teaching at nearby Hickory Grove School while he was still at Wesleyan. At age 21, he decided he wanted to be a school superintendent. He wrote application letters to school boards all over Iowa, outlining his personal history, enclosing some recommendations and declaring that he needed an annual salary of $600 to $1,200. Among the 30 replies, he received four solid job offers. Among them were a $720-a-year offer from the Algona board and a $1,000 bid from the board at DeWitt. Despite the smaller salary, Cowles chose Algona, saying later: "I guess it was because Algona was a county seat and had more of a pioneer appeal." He also was influenced by the town's rapid growth and its New England heritage.

Beginning the job in 1882 and performing the duties of superintendent, Cowles held the title of principal of the Algona school, which was staffed by nine women. Cowles sounded out the board about starting a high school, saying he would need an assistant if secondary education were begun. The board voted to set up a high school, but refused to hire an additional person. Two elementary classes were merged and a teacher was freed to serve as Cowles's assistant. The aide turned out to be Florence Call, daughter of a widely known Algona pioneer, banker Ambrose Call. In six months, Gardner Cowles and Florence — Cowles called her Flora — were engaged. On Dec. 3, 1884, the Rev. William Cowles performed the couple's wedding ceremony in the home of Florence's parents.

In 1883, while he held the school job, Gardner Cowles bought a half-interest in *The Algona Republican,* a weekly published by Milton Starr. And that is where his future partner, Harvey Ingham, came in, with a Page One editorial in *his* weekly, *The Upper Des Moines,* accusing Cowles of "threatening to neglect the pupils of the town to make a few dollars on a second-rate newspaper."

Cowles did make money on *The Republican,* managing the business affairs of the paper so well that partner Starr realized as much profit from his half-ownership as he previously had made when he was sole proprietor. Cowles called Starr "one of the poorest businessmen I've ever known." Not surprisingly the partnership lasted only about a year, with Cowles selling his interest back to Starr after a fight came up over a judgeship. "It seemed to me perfectly foolish for *The Republican* to take any bitter position in the case," Cowles said, but Starr insisted on getting into the scrap. For his part, Cowles insisted on retiring from the paper.

Like Cowles, Harvey Ingham was born before the Civil War — on Sept. 8, 1858 in a log cabin near Black Cat Creek north of Algona. He was the oldest of eight children of a New York native named William H. Ingham, who had started west for the California gold fields but got no farther than the prairie and forest lands of Kossuth County. He settled there in 1855 among the county's 300 other white citizens.

William Ingham lost all his money in the depression of 1857, staged a quick comeback, then moved his family to Algona in 1865, when Harvey was seven years old and the town's population was about 250. Like William Cowles, William Ingham was a sturdy pioneer individualist, whose code read: "If every man takes care of himself, the world is well cared for."

Harvey Ingham's mother, Caroline Rice Ingham, also a New Yorker, was much better educated than her husband, who had only a "common school" education in contrast to her training at New York's Fairfield Academy. A former schoolteacher, Mrs. Ingham wrote poetry and news copy for county newspapers and worked as an assistant editor.

During the Midwest's Indian unrest of the early 1860s, Caroline Ingham took little Harvey into hiding in the wilds. In 1862 and 1863, after Indians reportedly killed 737 settlers in Minnesota, alarmed frontier families fled to safe places like Fort Defiance, near Estherville, where the Inghams found refuge. No attacks materialized; in fact, no whites were reported killed in Iowa after the "Spirit Lake Massacre," in March, 1857, in which about two-score whites were slain. During the early 1860s, Harvey's father commanded the militia at Fort Defiance and remained there a year, acquiring the title "Captain," which he kept for life.

Frontier perils aside, the Ingham home was a stimulating place, with "plenty of high thinking" at the home fireside, Harvey Ingham said. "Some mighty problems of theology have been threshed out there," he recalled in later life. "Great reforms have been encouraged. Temperance, woman suffrage, freedom of religious opinion — all have had their friendly advocacy in turn."

Big-name lecturers who spoke in Algona — individuals like feminists Susan B. Anthony and Elizabeth Cady Stanton and a noted clergyman, philosopher and editor, Bishop Joseph Haven — often stayed in the Ingham home, bringing to the household "a broad outlook into world affairs," Ingham said. "The old home and the frontier united to teach a real democracy," he explained. " 'Will he work and is he honest?' was the test imposed by society as well as the business community in those primitive days."

From the home came "an abiding confidence in the essential integrity of human nature," and out of that background Harvey Ingham grew into a quick and wide-ranging reader (he frequently skimmed two and three books in a day) and developed a broad spectrum of intellectual interests.

A curious American tradition requires that any young boy who admits to intellectual interests also must be something less than ideally behaved — to counter suspicions of being prissy, if nothing else. Harvey qualified as a "terror" as well as a good student; when he was 11, he "jumped through an open schoolhouse window like a cricket when the teacher went to chastise him for some ludicrous answer he had given."

When he was 12, Harvey Ingham entered Algona's old Methodist College. Said Ingham: "Professor Baker immediately started me on Greek, Latin and geometry. Whatever talent I had fitted in with the program and I have gone through life along the lines laid down when I was a small boy."

In 1872, Harvey's father refused to vote for the re-election of President Ulysses S. Grant, the regular Republican candidate whose administration had a record of corruption. Instead, the elder Ingham backed Horace Greeley, nominee of the Democrats and Liberal Republicans, and that was rank heresy in strongly Republican north Iowa in the post-Civil War era. "Both the elder and younger Ingham felt the town's displeasure," historian W.C. Dewel said, "and the spitefulness of many who opposed his father made young Ingham into a potential maverick," even though William

Ingham suffered no lasting damage, becoming a well-to-do banker and landowner.

When Harvey Ingham was 18, in 1876, he took a long railroad trip to Philadelphia for the national centennial observance, riding four days and four nights, sleeping in his seat. He dated his observations on the case for racial equality from a long conversation with a black youth riding the same train.

After the Philadelphia trip, Ingham enrolled in the University of Iowa at Iowa City, where he was graduated in liberal arts in 1880, and where in 1881 he won his law degree. On campus, he was regarded as "a debater without equal." A classmate and friend, Frank O. Lowden, later governor of Illinois and in 1920 a major but unsuccessful contender for the Republican nomination for president, said young Ingham "could debate any question on either side equally well, whether he knew anything about it or not."

"This," Lowden added, "was not said in criticism but only in admiration of Harvey's marvelous resources. He was the most delightful and dearest opponent I ever had in an argument."

Ingham also developed considerable skill in shooting pool, which he made a lifetime pastime.

He began his career as a newspaper writer in 1879, while he was a student, writing editorials for a collegiate publication called *The Vidette.*

Ingham practiced law in Cedar Rapids for a year, then moved back to Algona in 1882, intending to continue his law career there. At the same time, Al Hudson, half-owner of *The Upper Des Moines,* wanted to sell out and move to Sioux City. Hudson convinced Ingham that a couple of years of newspapering might be useful in developing a law practice. Ingham bought Hudson's interest in the paper — but never got back to law.

"Harvey Ingham became a journalist by choice — almost by instinct," wrote one of his longtime associates in an editorial at Ingham's death in 1949. "He frequently said that he had found, for him, the happiest of vocations. He loved it; he was designed for it."

An eager editor from the start, he felt what one commentator called "an apostolic urge to better the manners and thought of mankind." He was, over the years, to become a sought-after consultant and adviser to individuals who preferred a man who shed light rather than heat on issues. In a eulogy he composed to honor another distinguished

Iowan, he summed up his own philosophy of service: "How can a man better serve the light of his times than by guiding his fellows into better ways of thinking, better forms of administration and a more intelligent appraisal of themselves and others?"

Not surprisingly, after their first confrontation, Ingham the young editor and Cowles the young school superintendent developed a close friendship at Algona. Said W. C. Dewel in his unpublished history of *The Register*:

"They were young men of much higher type than the common herd. Moreover, they were fellow graduate collegians ... in a day when collegians and graduates were scarce, and they were alike ambitious to achieve distinction."

Cowles, after leaving his newspaper and school posts in 1884, went into business with his banker-father-in-law. Ambrose Call held contracts for running mail wagons from railroad stations to towns without train service in Iowa, Kansas and the Dakotas. The Call-Cowles firm contracted with the government to serve more than 30 such routes. Cowles's experience in this field was to serve him in expanding his newspapers' reach across Iowa.

Cowles also opened a farm loan business, seizing the main chance at an ideal time for making money on fertile north Iowa farms that had been wilderness only a quarter-century before. His first big deal involved him in the sale of 1,000 acres of land, a transaction in which the seller asked $4 an acre and agreed to pay a commission of 25 cents an acre; the agent with the listing offered to split the commission with Cowles if he found a buyer. Cowles, who realized he was being offered the land for $3.87½ an acre, hurried off to Des Moines, where he talked a loan company into taking a half-interest with him in the property. A year later, Cowles sold the 1,000 acres for $8 an acre.

After paying costs and taxes, Cowles was left with a clear profit of $1,800 — and a sense of wonder. "For a fellow who never had handled much money in his life, that $1,800 was so wonderful that I counted it over and over," he said. "I was so nervous with it in my hands that I hardly knew what to do with it."

Other loans and profitable deals followed and the next step, inevitably, was banking. Cowles became heavily interested in a string of some 10 banks in Kossuth and Emmet Counties, becoming president of the major bank of the chain, the County Savings Bank of Algona, Kossuth's seat.

Those who knew Cowles said that in his Algona years he reached a net worth of $200,000, an extraordinary amount for the times. But he never worked as a day-by-day banker and his banking interests were so widely scattered that he once was embarrassed in Chicago when he drafted a $5,000 check on one of his banks and wrote the bank's name incorrectly on the check form. It was not characteristic of the meticulous Cowles.

Harvey Ingham's acquaintanceship also was widening, partly because he was such an entertaining speaker. His paper was entertaining and lively, too, and that attracted increasing attention in governmental and Republican party circles, to which both weekly editor Ingham and banker Cowles had gravitated.

From his father, Gardner Cowles had inherited an interest in public affairs and Republican politics. When he was 27, Cowles began attracting political attention, plunging into the middle of one of the longest and liveliest Iowa GOP convention battles in the state's history, in which Jonathan P. Dolliver, a rising young Fort Dodge lawyer, sought the convention's nomination for Congress.

(Iowa Republican politics were no simple thing; the convolutions, involutions and revolutions within various factions might be compared with the intraparty machinations of the national Democratic organization of the 1950s and 1960s. At the turn of the century in Iowa, it was Standpatter versus Progressive, and the complications boggled the mind.)

The year was 1888, the place Webster City; Cowles was secretary of the convention, despite a run-in with A. A. Brunson, head of Kossuth County's Republican organization and backer of Congressman Adoniram J. Holmes of Boone, who wanted to be renominated. To be named a delegate, Cowles had to agree to support Holmes, though he favored Dolliver. On the 110th ballot, Dolliver won the nomination and went on to win election to Congress and ultimately to become one of the nation's great U.S. senators.

Cowles and Brunson tangled again over a postmastership in Algona, but Cowles's man won, and Cowles kept his hand in county politics. In 1899, at age 38, he was elected Kossuth County representative to the 1900 Iowa Legislature.

In Des Moines, Cowles again found himself on the political hotseat, supporting U.S. Senator John Gear, a member of the party's Standpat wing, seeking re-election in

1900. Gear was opposed by the state's leading Progressive Republican, Albert B. Cummins. When Cowles voted for Gear — state legislatures elected U.S. senators until 1913 — Cummins forces vowed to block any Cowles return to the Iowa House. Cowles took that as a challenge, won a close election and returned to the capital. His liking for Des Moines grew while he spent another three months there in the 1902 Legislature.

Politics intrigued Harvey Ingham, too, and his connections with GOP politicians won him an appointment to the Algona postmastership, which he held from 1898 to 1902, grossing $2,000 a year. In 1900, he became sole owner of *The Upper Des Moines* and appeared to be riding high in his roles as editor, postmaster, and member of the University of Iowa's own Board of Regents, appointed to a six-year term in 1896.

But by mid-1902, Ingham was ready to pull up stakes, having run into difficulty with the Progressives when he and Cowles decided to support Standpatter Gear. The problem with the Progressives was compounded when Ingham in 1900 sought the Republican nomination for Congress from the old Tenth (North Iowa) district and ran in a marathon convention against 10 other candidates. Cowles was Ingham's floor manager and neither endeared himself to the Progressives when the result of their operations in the convention was the nomination of James P. Conner of Denison. Conner — a fellow townsman of Iowa Gov. Leslie Shaw, a Standpat leader — went on to defeat the Democratic nominee in the 1900 election and subsequently to serve five congressional terms.

Ingham also ran into trouble supporting Cowles for his second term as a state representative, and anti-Ingham sentiment encouraged the establishment in 1901 of a new Republican newspaper in Algona, *The Advance*. The intention was to hurt Ingham's business. The move gave the town of 3,000 population four weeklies, three of them Republican — Ingham's *Upper Des Moines,* and *The Republican* and *The Advance*. The fourth, *The Courier,* was Democratic. As the competition ate into Ingham's profits, he was defeated for re-election to the regents post. Deep in troubles, Ingham in the late spring of 1902 sold his paper to *The Republican* after having received a telegram at 10 o'clock one spring morning offering him an editorship at *The Des Moines Register and Leader*. He wired acceptance at 1 p.m. and was off on his Des Moines adventure.

A year and a half later, in late 1903, Gardner Cowles, who was 42 years old, followed the 45-year-old Harvey Ingham down to Des Moines, determined to help Ingham pull his chestnuts — among them a $24,500 stock investment — out of the fire on *The Register and Leader,* which was losing ground to its competition.

After 16 months as editor, Ingham felt he had failed to re-establish *The Register and Leader* in Des Moines' competitive newspaper field. During that period, the paper was owned by George Roberts, an Iowan who was director of the U.S. Mint, and Samuel Strauss, who had been publisher of *The Leader* before its merger with *The Register.* Ingham and Cowles had long since talked about trying to acquire the paper, with Cowles designated as rejuvenator of the publishing and business end as well as supplier of much-needed capital.

They made their move at a time when a quiet revolution was beginning to take place in American journalism, a movement by newspapers away from political orientation and toward public service. They became a forward-thrusting team that galvanized and changed Iowa journalism in the first half of the Twentieth Century. But for one week in 1903 their future partnership was in doubt.

Cowles and Ingham nearly missed their chance when a financial monkey wrench was thrown into the works on Sunday, Nov. 1, 1903. George Roberts agreed to sell *The Register and Leader* to three prominent Iowa Republicans, F. L. Maytag, then a farm machinery manufacturer at Newton, Iowa; James Smith, a well-off Osage lumber dealer, and A. B. Funk, a newspaper editor at Spirit Lake.

The announcement of sale caught Harvey Ingham flat-footed; he feared his editing job was lost to Funk and that he also might lose part of his financial investment. Ingham wrote to Cowles, telling him that technicalities still stood in the way of completion of the sale and that if Cowles could put either $75,000 or $50,000 into the paper, he could control it himself or in partnership with Ingham. Cowles made the 128-mile train trip to Des Moines, conferred with the Roberts group, went home and talked the matter over with his wife, Florence — as he was to do all his life when dealing with major projects — and decided to act.

On Nov. 7, *The Register and Leader* carried the startling announcement that the sale to Maytag, Smith and Funk had, "upon mature consideration proved to be impractical," had been canceled and Gardner Cowles had become a new stockholder.

Cowles had bought 1,500 shares, 50 per cent of the outstanding stock, and with that he and Ingham had taken control of the paper, jointly owning 2,045 of the 3,000 outstanding shares. No price was announced at the time, but years later Cowles said the figure was a little less than $45 a share, or about $67,000. A few months before, Ingham also had paid about $45 a share for his stock purchase. Within a few months, Cowles bought the rest of the outstanding Roberts and Strauss holdings for $45.83 a share — $43,800 — for a total investment of $111,000, plus assuming some of the paper's unpaid bills.

Cowles had watched the progress of *The Register and Leader* during his two House sessions. "Both Harvey and I always had the feeling that it was possible to build a strong daily newspaper in Des Moines," Cowles said. "We probably throught more of the opportunity than of the discouraging condition of *The Register and Leader*. And I always felt that Des Moines as the state capital and the state's largest city was a desirable place in which to locate."

When the opportunity came, investor Cowles was ready with the necessary cash, having submitted farm-loan requests to a Chicago investment house and arranged to borrow on his Kossuth County farmland holdings. "These applications were promptly accepted and the loans were closed," Cowles once explained. "I really had no pressing need for the money, but it seemed to be a good thing to do on the theory that something would arise . . . . I simply held the checks or drafts in my safe. The fact that I had this idle money was a factor in my making up my mind to buy *The Register and Leader*."

2 EARLY EXPECTATIONS

In 1904, Gardner Cowles moved his wife and family to Des Moines (pop. 72,000) from Algona (pop. 3,000). The family, which included sons Russell, John and Gardner (Mike) jr., and daughters Helen, Florence and Bertha, moved to an "expensive" $60-a-month house on Seventeenth Street north of Woodland Avenue.

Cowles then set about dealing with the formidable problems at *The Register and Leader*. Staff morale and salaries were low, employee turnover was high and the newspaper's financial problems were sizable.

The Register and Leader was widely known and respected in Iowa even though its influence had begun fading. It held sway as the morning paper, facing advertising and circulation competiton from the city's three afternoon papers, *The Capital, The News* and *The Tribune*. When *Register and Leader* financial losses continued, Cowles ordered a 3 per cent assessment on all outstanding stock in January, 1904 and another 1 per cent in June. Samuel Strauss and George Roberts soon sold out their shares to Cowles and Ingham, and by July, 1904, eight months after he had taken over, Cowles had the paper in the black. Sometimes he managed that only by such stratagems as putting off buying two typewriters, thus turning a "profit" for one bookkeeping period. Since then, the organization never has had to use red ink, even in the depths of the 1930s Great Depression.

Cowles revived his paper's flagging spirits by being fair, tough and exacting — using his well-developed ability for dealing with the intricacies of business to create financially secure elbow room for his colleague Harvey Ingham. The security permitted Ingham to approach the editorial side of the newspaper with the kind of flexible rules that allowed his editors and writers leeway to experiment, to explore and to develop a newspaper that would reflect the broad variety of American and Iowa life.

Despite the obvious financial problems, Cowles got into the newspaper business at a favorable time, when interest in news had expanded as the United States grew into a world power after the Spanish-American War and when merchants were discovering the advantages of large-scale advertising. In a few years, the new auto industry would generate even more advertising.

Cowles's long suit was management, the ability to make the business part of the newspaper profession work, finding new markets, discovering ways to get a better product to more customers. Jay Norwood (Ding) Darling, one of America's greatest cartoonists and a long-time *Register* employee, summed up those qualities in an acknowledgement he wrote not long before his death in 1962. Listing individuals to whom he owed "a debt of gratitude," Darling said: "Chief among them was Gardner Cowles the elder, who rescued *The Des Moines Register* and me at about the same time from the oblivion of mediocrity. He showered upon us the rich rewards of his unique and quite revolutionary methods of newspaper management, traditions which have been maintained by his successors, John and Gardner, jr., and I like to think that the editorial freedom, independent of censorship from above, set a new standard of dignity and responsibility for editorial cartoonists who were to follow."

Darling was a singular example of how the *Register* approach worked. For 40 years, his spot was staked out in the middle of Page One of *The Register,* and the rules were that he could draw what he wanted on any topic, important or incidental. Winner of two Pulitzer Prizes — in 1924 and 1943 — he could thrive at *The Register* because of the extent of his freedom. All that Publisher Cowles asked was that Darling be honest with himself. The upshot of that was that sometimes drawings took a position directly opposite the viewpoint on the editorial page. There was, for example, the day in 1916 when Darling on Page One advocated U.S. preparedness for war (World War I was deep into trench warfare) while an editorial expressed the contrary view.

Darling went his way and Editor Harvey Ingham went his, and Darling once described the situation this way: "I do not consult my editorial chief and I never have. My convictions may not be worth much to the world, but they are my own, and if I'm going through life expressing anybody's convictions, they are going to be my own."

Keeping the peace between the conservative Darling and the moderate-liberal Ingham was one of Cowles's most difficult problems. At one point, said Cowles's son, John, "Ding began to think his judgment was as good or better than Harvey's. Ding became increasingly critical and the issue reached Gardner Cowles. He told Darling: 'Jay, you are doing fine as a cartoonist, you stick to that and let Harvey run the editorial page.' Ding commented: 'That's pretty sloppy stuff Harvey is putting out in his editorials.' "

John Cowles went on: "Harvey in turn didn't like many of the cartoons Ding was drawing and Gardner had to soften up Harvey by saying: 'You have complete latitude on the editorial page. You do whatever you want, say whatever you want, but remember that Jay Darling is a valuable member of the team.' Gardner intermittently had to placate either Harvey or Ding to keep them in the harness together."

Darling and the Cowleses usually got along well, but there were times when disagreements spread a coldness that stopped conversation entirely. That sometimes forced the late Basil (Stuffy) Walters, managing editor in the 1930s, to serve as a mediator and information conduit. "There would be differences of opinion about the views expressed in Ding's cartoons," Walters recalled. "I would not say the Cowleses were mad at him, just uncomfortable. Ding would say: 'Would you please tell Mike [Gardner Cowles, jr.] this or that?' I would, and then I would report back." Strained relations never lasted long because Darling was so highly regarded in the Cowles domain.

Another observer saw Cowles as a molding force, declaring: "Gardner Cowles was an educator of men, and demanded results. To get them, you had to know what you were doing — to learn. By turning the spotlight on one activity after another, he kept all employees alert. This discipline had the power of almost unwittingly turning drifters into men filled with a purpose. Ordinary men who had the capacity to learn were transformed into extraordinary workers."

His goal was to instill in each employee a feeling that he was an important cog, a key individual.

Early in the operation, increased advertising revenue gave Cowles the opportunity to spend sizable sums on improving news coverage and content. In 1911, historian Johnson Brigham wrote that Cowles and Ingham had made *The Register and Leader* a "great metropolitan daily with its news, editorial, financial and amusement departments at an expense undreamed of in the 1890s."

Cowles gained esteem both in and out of the organization by his insistence on honesty in the paper's business affairs as well as in handling the news. In the early days, when money problems were still severe, a railroad attorney told Cowles that the paper had secretly been on the railroad's payroll for some time. The railroad, he said, was willing to continue the payments. Cowles checked the books, discovered that *The Register and Leader* was receiving a rail subsidy and ended it.

Cowles was too keen a businessman to have been deceived about the general condition of the newspaper when he bought it in 1903, but he may have been misled by assurances that circulation was 32,000 copies daily. Actually, circulation was only about 14,000, of which probably not more than 8,000 copies went to paid-up subscribers or buyers from newsboys in the street. Newspapers then did not always tell the truth about circulation.

The padded figures led to two confrontations. First, the paper's business manager asked Cowles to claim the 32,000 figure in a statement that was to be sent to the firm's advertising agent in Chicago. When Cowles refused to sign the statement, the business manager suggested that someone else in authority could sign it.

"I'll not ask anybody to do something that I won't do," Cowles replied. "We'll just not issue a circulation statement at present." His adamant attitude upset the business manager; thousands of dollars' worth of advertising contracts hung in the balance because ad rates are paid for partly on the basis of circulation totals.

When Cowles went to Chicago to impress upon the advertising agent that he would not issue false figures, the agent told him to get himself another representative — which Cowles did.

Another time, Cowles commented on the dilemma: "Requests from advertising agencies in New York and Chicago were mighty embarrassing when they asked for sworn, detailed circulation statements. All I could do was forget to send them what they asked for." For a long time, circulation and payment problems continued. At one point, Cowles told his son John that he had found 2,000 to 3,000 so-called subscribers on the books who had gotten out of the habit of paying for the paper.

"Many people, including some extremely prominent Des Moines people, hadn't paid for two or three years," John Cowles said. "After a month or two, my father's collectors had only been able to succeed with about half these accounts. My father ordered all the unpaid subscriptions to be dropped immediately."

Irate readers besieged Publisher Cowles with protests. "Many of them were leading Des Moines businessmen who told my father that he was questioning their credit and financial solvency," John Cowles said. "My father told them that they could restore *their* credit and financial solvency in his mind if they would pay their back bills and keep up to date in the future.... Most of them did, but many didn't."

Though he was a son of a Methodist minister, Cowles refused to give the paper free to clergymen. "Many men of the cloth violently protested," John Cowles said. "They felt that, since they were working for God, they should receive the paper free. My father said he sympathized with their financial plight but that they should pay for their subscriptions if they wanted the paper, just like anyone else."

The paper began compiling gains, but it was not until 1906 that Cowles could issue a sworn statement saying that circulation had passed 25,000. Meanwhile, he reduced some expenses while continuing to improve the paper.

Today's worldly wise — and the sophisticates of his own day — might view Cowles's use of maxims as simplistic, but he meant it when he posted a sign saying:

"Things don't just happen. Somebody makes them happen."

Harvey Ingham was one of the major doers in Cowles's life as well as a pivotal figure in the history of journalism in Iowa. Onetime Vice-President and former Iowan Henry A. Wallace summed him up as a transitional figure:

"Harvey Ingham in his life, more than anyone I know, represented a conscious living bridge between the rugged pioneer individualism of early Iowa and the complex national and international problems of an Iowa approaching maturity."

Although he was instrumental, early, in confining editorial comment to the editorial pages, Ingham felt obliged in his first year in Des Moines, when George Roberts and Samuel Strauss owned *The Register and*

Leader, to emphasize his loyalty to the Republican Party. He was on a "Republican" paper and politics was still a major factor in newspaper life. Republicans, he wrote, had a duty to "preserve the country from experiment and alarm," but he didn't hesitate to say a good word for an Iowa City Democrat, Judge Martin Wade, who had just been elected to Congress. Calling Wade "an able lawyer," Ingham wrote: "As long as Iowa wants to send a Democrat, it could not have picked a more creditable representative."

Later, in 1909, he wrote: "Sometimes it becomes important in the accomplishment of public ends the newspaper believes in to have certain men win. Then the newspaper properly supports the man. But when the fortunes of the individual and the cause are not identical, then the office-seeker is nothing whatsoever to the newspaper."

The Cowles-Ingham effort to separate editorial opinion from news coverage was a continuing goal. It was not always achieved, of course. Opinion sometimes slipped into the reporting and positioning of news stories; subeditors and reporters are always conscious of an editor's or the publisher's preferences among news topics and news figures. Sometimes issues of public importance demanded, in Cowles's and Ingham's eyes, coverage in the news columns that by its nature stated a position — as in *The Register and Leader*'s attacks on civic corruption. The goal was, and is, to avoid "slanting" and to present a news subject in as full, clear and honest a light as reporters and editors can summon up. That they sometimes fail is no surprise; that they succeed in achieving true, balanced coverage as often as they do is.

Ingham's far-ranging humanism, his expansiveness of character, his "liberalism" in the sense of openness to change and tolerance for and encouragement of diversity and variety account for much of the success of his and Cowles's newspaper adventure.

Ingham was a true opinion leader, often far in advance of a sizable proportion of his readership. From his first years in Des Moines, he opposed racism, attacked war as savage and futile, promoted international courts and international law projects, and all his life spoke up for the underprivileged, especially children. In 1903, deep in the heart of capitalist territory, he even braved critics with an editorial saluting labor unions, something that not many editors were doing in those days. "No thoughtful student of the times can fail to recognize that labor unionism has come to stay," he wrote. "Labor not only has the same right to organize that capital has, but labor has shown that many of the same advantages accrue to society from organization of one as from organization of the other. . . . Labor organization dignifies labor, protects those who are illy able to protect themselves, and makes independent — therefore courageous, ambitious and substantial — the men who do the manual work of the world."

In the redhot battle against corruption in Des Moines' City Hall in 1906 and 1907, Ingham — noted as a speaker — took to airing his views from one of his favorite places, the back platform of the Center Street streetcar. Years later, a friend wrote Harvey about those speeches: "In stentorian tones you told us all about it. I have passed up a [street]car because your figure wasn't on the back platform. I wanted to hear you talk. You never lacked an audience."

Never afraid to join in battles against abuses by big business and entrenched wealth, Ingham strongly supported the campaigns in 1906 to eliminate contaminated meat from American dinner tables and to regulate the meatpackers, the railroads and the insurance companies.

"Packers should take the best and most stringent inspection law Congress can frame," he advised. "They will be forced to take it in the end."

An ardent backer of President Theodore Roosevelt in T.R.'s anti-trust battles against the big-money interests, Ingham wrote boldly: "Predatory wealth is not a fiction of excited imagination. Resistance to regulation is not something conjured up to scare the innocent. . . . President Roosevelt . . . lifted the banner of popular rights. . . . The American people will never again view with quite the same complacency some of the methods of large finance."

In 1911, Ingham wrote his approval of a court decision to dissolve the tobacco trust. He declared: "It is not so much an object of the people now to prevent big business as it is to have big business done under such supervision as will insure fair play and a reasonable division of the benefits." In 1914, he praised the Sherman Anti-Trust Act as "one of the shortest, most comprehensive and effective statutes ever written," and saluted Henry Ford for boosting wages in his automobile plant from $2.40 a day to a daily minimum of $5. Reporting that more than 50 Ford workers had gotten married after the raise went into effect, Ingham wrote that the workers had been waiting "for a reasonable guarantee against misfortune." He added: "A guarantee against the future plays an important part in developing the best citizenship."

He was a free enterprise man from the beginning — and he was the kind of free-enterpriser who was not only willing but also eager to spread the wealth around. Down the years, he was consistent, showing his colors in the deepening Depression. In 1931 he warned: "Capitalism, if it is to survive, has this one lesson to learn, that all human organization, whether in business or government, is for the purpose of bringing its benefits to all of the people.... Resentment is bound to be bred by an assumption of exclusive right on the part of the so-called 'upper classes' and resentment is one of the most dominating and most deadly of human motives. It is the business of capital to see that resentment is not bred among the masses.... Holders of great, accumulated wealth of the United States are not monarchs in the making. They, more than anybody else, are public servants."

He repeatedly stressed "fair play" and never let up in his fight for equal treatment for black people and for other non-white races. Discussing the plight of blacks, Ingham wrote: "I have seen at every athletic contest of the state paths carefully marked that colored boys might run unobstructed. I have yet to learn of a colored boy who left an athletic contest feeling that he might have won and was not permitted to win. Can you name another competition in life where that is true?"

With Cowles's approval, Ingham fought against racial discrimination during a period when race prejudice was widespread and strong and when his liberal attitude was unpopular among thousands of white Iowans. He did not falter — it was perhaps his calm and logical approach to problems of intolerance that took some of the heat out of the controversies. Coolly and sympathetically he insisted that human beings all should treat each other as human beings — in the phrase that became a litany later — regardless of color, religion or national origin.

A relentless, unyielding optimism pervaded Ingham's life. In 1946, after a long war in which humanity only just triumphed over inhumanity, he could, at the age of 88, still see progress: "The ancient Greeks were the most scholarly people in history. They had a remarkable architecture and literature.... Yet the ancient Greeks came and went. You and I can't know what is happening to us. Extinction has happened to four or five races of people. But I am not pessimistic. We have progressed thus far. I think we will continue to go ahead."

3 "GETTING GOING"

Business progress for *The Register and Leader* was something that had to wait for the Cowles touch. Harvey Ingham and George Roberts merely produced a good newspaper and hoped for the best, failing to sense or heed the need for concentration on sales. Cowles saw the potentialities for a state paper full of news of state-wide interest. Ingham eventually took the lesson, telling a country-editor friend: "It does you no good in a business way just to put out a good paper; you also have to go out and sell it."

As the seat of state government and the news center of Iowa, Des Moines offered a great opportunity for developing a state newspaper. Iowa farmers and small-town residents looked on the capital as the state's big-league territory. The community's reputation as a "sin city" — the description was deserved — didn't hurt its fascination quotient either.

Not many small-town residents read dailies then, getting their news instead from weeklies; so did farmers, who also read the agricultural papers. Although some "outside" daily papers came into the state, "Iowa was practically virgin territory for a newspaper circulation genius," one account said. Northern Iowa, it said, was served by Chicago, Minneapolis and St. Paul papers. Chicago papers dominated eastern Iowa, "where Des Moines papers were scarcely known," and competed "even to the very doorstep of the Des Moines papers." Western Iowa "was served to some extent by Omaha and Sioux City papers, yet all the circulation put together did not give state coverage."

The competing *Des Moines News,* which claimed 45,000 circulation, and *The Capital,* which said it sold 37,000 papers daily, were concerned more with cutting each other's throats in the evening field than with the small morning competition offered by *The Register and Leader* and the pallid existence of the third evening paper, *The Tribune.* The greeting to Cowles from *The Capital* was nonchalant: "We welcome Gardner Cowles as one of our 'hated' rivals and we wish him success," the editors said. The nonchalance evaporated as the Cowles-Ingham paper made inroads into the other papers' already-suspect circulation figures.

Readers found *The News* breezy and more interesting-looking than *The Capital* but scattershot and weighed down by numerous "canned" pictures received by mail in "mat" form. *The News,* which belonged to the Clover Leaf chain of midwestern dailies, was regarded as an outsider and never seemed to have put roots deep into the city's life.

The Capital used a red banner headline across its Page One each day but otherwise looked heavy and unattractive, carrying few photographs and no cartoons and concentrating on national and political news. Other drawbacks to its becoming a true general-interest local paper included its use of advertising on the editorial page and its reputation as an old-line Republican sheet that generally hewed to the party's policies.

Though he belonged to the Republican Party and supported GOP candidates, Gardner Cowles did not want his newspaper centering on Republican promotion or devoting a lot of space to advancing the cause of individual candidates. He wanted to produce a successful paper.

Cowles was unlike his most famous newspaper predecessor in Des Moines, James (Ret) Clarkson, a member of the "Fighting Clarkson" family and a staunch Republican who used the pages of his *Register* to promote the cause of the GOP. "We give to the Republican party all the power we have, and take nothing from it," Clarkson wrote in 1886. Competition was fierce that year. *The Register* was up against four other dailies, *The Leader, The Capital, The News* and *The Blade.*

Cyrenus Cole, a *Register* reporter in the Clarkson era as well as a sometime Cedar Rapids editor, a notable Iowa congressman and a historian, succinctly described the partisan newspapering in Clarkson's day. He wrote: "The style of journalism of which Ret Clarkson was a chief exponent was already on the way out. It was a personal and political journalism. The journalism that superseded it was not written on the editorial page but was spread out over the news pages in the form of unbiased information from which readers could formulate their own conclusions and opinions."

Ret Clarkson continued his newspaper career a few more years, then accepted a Washington appointment as assistant postmaster general and sold out to his business-manager-brother, Dick, who edited the paper until he sold it in 1902.

The stories of the "Fighting Clarksons" and their *Register* and of the state's pioneer printers are worthy of a book themselves. Such a history would include papers like *The Iowa State Register*, which began in 1857, and Barlow Granger's *Iowa Star,* launched in 1849.

This, however, is the story of the Twentieth Century *Register,* which "really got going," Gardner Cowles always said, in 1908 and 1909.

On the news side, *The Register and Leader* was already moving against the corruption that bedeviled Des Moines' city government, which, one historian wrote, "probably had the worst reputation for rottenness and inefficiency of any administration in the history of Des Moines." The capital had gambling houses that ran "practically wide open," this account said, and "prostitution was virtually protected by the police, the prostitutes being herded into police court every month or two, fined $10 each and sent back to carry on their trade until the next roundup." Meanwhile, ward aldermen frequently collected payoffs on business that was done with city government.

In a *Register and Leader* crusade against "the City Hall gang," Ingham appeared on public platforms around Des Moines urging adoption of a reform program. Jay Darling's cartoons — both on Page One and on the editorial page — came out swinging. Out front, a five-column cartoon asked: "Which side are you going to line up with?" Characterized on one side was a procession of upstanding citizens demonstrating support of a commission form of city government that required that the mayor and four council members be chosen at large in nonpartisan elections. Represented on the other side was a disreputable-looking array of characters favoring the old "city misgovernment." Referring to a ballot proposal to build a new City Hall, one of the worst-looking characters was depicted saying: "Turn your money over to us. We will build you the best $50,000 City Hall you ever saw for $300,000."

The anti-corruption drive resulted in a victory at the polls June 20, 1907. The citizenry voted to throw out the boss-ridden ward system and set up the commission plan. No city official could be personally interested in city contracts and a civil service commission was set up to hire city workers on the basis of merit rather than political patronage. Candidates also were required to file accounts of campaign spending and its sources. The reforms also included provision for recalling city officials before their terms expired. In addition, voters could decide by ballot whether certain proposed ordinances should become law.

In 1908, after long argument, a civic group agreed on a slate of candidates for mayor and the four council offices under the new commission setup. The slate won the backing of the newspaper — but not of the voters in the 1908 election.

Still, the reform itself produced a situation in which aldermen were no longer getting kickbacks on construction of city buildings and improvements, and city officials could no longer protect "the saloon interests," gamblers and prostitutes.

The 1908 election was not the only time that the Cowles-Ingham papers were on the losing side of an election, but Editor Ingham took the beating philosophically. He wrote: "The people will not always accept the judgment of a civic league or good-government club, just as a jury will not always accept the view of an able and honest lawyer. But that is no cause for discouragement. The people are more likely to be right than not. They do not often make serious blunders. The good lawyer does not quit because one verdict has been rendered against him. He goes to the next case with renewed zeal." Through the years, Ingham and the paper renewed their zeal repeatedly, policing government at all levels.

That first decade was filled with other news events that *The Register and Leader* covered, from the digging of the Panama Canal, which started in 1903 and was completed in 1915, to the devastating spring 1903 flood on the Des Moines River (the coverage included an unusual eight-column, three-inch-deep panoramic photograph on Page One), to 1906's San Francisco earthquake and fire, in which more than 450 persons died, to Adm. Robert E. Peary's 1909 discovery of the location of the North Pole, to a major fire in 1904 that threatened to destroy Iowa's golden-domed Capitol. Although firemen and volunteers saved it from destruction, the Statehouse building suffered damage estimated at $300,000 to $500,000.

In 1906, Ingham took up the cudgel for full rights for blacks after an incident involving a black minister from Philadelphia. The central figure was the Rev. Matthew Anderson, who was attending the national assembly of the Presbyterian Church in Des Moines, the first time since the Civil War that the church's northern and southern branches met together.

Dr. Anderson, an alumnus of Princeton University, was invited to attend a Princeton banquet at the Chamberlain Hotel in connection with the church meeting, then later was told he could not attend because objections had been raised to the presence of a black man.

Afterward, Dr. Anderson said that evidently the committee feared that the presence of a black might upset southern Presbyterians. *The Register and Leader* printed a long Page One story on the subject while the editorial page carried pictures of Dr. Anderson and an Ingham editorial that accused the Presbyterian assembly of condoning the action barring Dr. Anderson from the banquet. Ingham asked: "What is to be the effect on society when the church refuses to stand without flinching? . . . Can the great Presbyterian body compromise by saying that conduct must go with color either in this world or the next, and not lose all vital hold on the thought and conscience of men?"

The first couple of years on Cowles's side of the business were focused on regrouping. In only a few years the operation began to work effectively.

Railroad schedules and Sunday afternoon drives were keys to the steady circulation growth of *The Register and Leader* outside Des Moines. When Cowles took over, the railroads carried all of the newspapers destined for readers out in the state. Since automobiles and trucks had not yet arrived in numbers and there were no concrete highways, Cowles became an expert on railroad schedules. Without checking a schedule, he knew where each train traveling in Iowa was supposed to be at any hour, day or night. Knowing the timetables, he could design his paper's printing schedules to get the freshest news possible in a specific town's shipment of papers.

As train traffic declined and trucks and cars increased in great numbers, Cowles became an ardent and knowledgeable promoter of good highways. As a driver, he was not a success. In about 1908, after he had bought a big green Studebaker-Garford auto, he took it out on the street — and drove into the side of a streetcar that had halted to pick up passengers. Cowles escaped injury and neither car nor streetcar was damaged much, but the humiliated Cowles gave up driving. He assigned the job of handling his auto to the hired man who milked the cows kept in the barn back of the Cowles house. For the rest of his life, Cowles had a chauffeur take him where he wanted to drive.

Sunday afternoons, Florence and Gardner Cowles often took drives to nearby cities or towns. Cowles asked residents how they liked the Cowles product and whether delivery service was good. On Mondays, Cowles held conferences with his circulation chief to talk over the situation in the Sunday-drive town.

Cowles also attacked his circulation problems by recognizing that circulation men too often were like the era's "medicine men," using all kinds of trick schemes "guaranteed to attract readers like flies." Cowles did, however, let his circulation men experiment with offers of expensive premiums for subscriptions — "pots and pans, flatirons, kettles, skillets, books, pictures, free trips and assorted hardware." He hired several circulation managers, one account said, including "one wonder who put on great gains but never collected any money [and] another who came from the east, took one discouraged look, and departed without a word. He returned the keys to the office by mail without comment."

While Cowles tried out various circulation experts, a recruit from his home town, red-haired, energetic, optimistic and boisterous Bill Cordingley — who wore "the loudest clothes in town" — was working as a *Register and Leader* circulation department clerk. Cordingley had come down to Des Moines from Algona, where he had worked as a clerk in a grain elevator office and on the side had managed the Algona Brownies, an all-black baseball team.

Cordingley impressed Cowles with his ability to motivate fieldmen. Gradually the publisher turned increasing responsibilities over to Cordingley, in 1906 naming him circulation manager. He did a notable job, continuing until his death in 1946, but no small part of Cordingley's success stemmed from the fact that Cowles himself was such a good circulation man, thorough as well as inspired, always exercising considerable supervision over circulation projects. Cowles, Ingham, Cordingley and others in the newspaper "family" became convinced that they were putting out the finest paper in the state and one of the finest in the nation and they hired men with similar enthusiasm.

In 1902, before Cowles's move to Des Moines, *Register and Leader* editors had been pleased by a report showing that sales of competing Chicago papers in Des Moines had dropped 20 per cent in one period. The paper had improved, they insisted, and researchers who look at early copies of *The Register and Leader* find that they provided wide-ranging information, controversy and bright writing for the times.

Less than a year after he took over, Cowles had introduced a color comics section, a feature that typified influential Sunday newspapers in the early 1900s. Announcing the addition on Sept. 17, 1904, the editors said they thought that the "rather expensive venture into a new field will prove successful" and that the new section cost as much as either of the two other syndicated sets of color comics sold to newspapers. (Though comics still retain their hold on readers, few of those features — "Herr Spiegleberger," "Simon Simple," and "Billy Bounce" — would be remembered even by old-timers.)

Jay Darling's cartoons helped increase the popularity of the paper after he joined the staff in 1906. Readers also liked the lively writing of the paper's knowledgeable drama critic, W. E. Anderson, whose pen name was Matelot, and who drew a sizable readership because Des Moines then was on a major theater circuit and the nation's big stage plays and musical comedies regularly played the Iowa capital.

Anderson's articles and stories, illustrated with pictures, sometimes filled a page in the Sunday paper. As his fame spread, a *New York Times* piece in 1904 called him "one of the few writers on theatrical matters outside New York whose opinions are worthy of reproduction." In London, a publication called *Free Lance* also praised Anderson, declaring that his drama page reflected "a wide knowledge of the drama and a critical spirit that is intensely modern."

Of a musical comedy titled "The Isle of Spice," Anderson gave this description: "A small body of antique jokes entirely surrounded by chorus girls." In 1905, he wrote one of the first Des Moines movie reviews, of a film consisting of newsreels in which the participants apparently strutted a lot. "Nothing really important ever can happen," he wrote, "unless the inevitable kinetoscope is in position to record in animated sequence the action that may take place. It would seem that the modern hero holds his deeds of valor in abeyance until the busy and sensitive cylinder begins to record him at the rate of 400 poses a minute."

Appealing to a different kind of reader was Joe Trigg's column, Farm Philosophy, consisting of miscellaneous information, opinion and attempts at quiet humor, some of which succeeded.

As with the fake circulation figures he first encountered, Cowles also was not impressed by the cheap prices at which the other Des Moines papers were being sold. *The News* was charging only seven cents a week for the six dailies and the Sunday paper it sold. By mail, *The News* cost $2 a year for the daily or $2.50 daily and Sunday. *The Capital* charged similar rates.

Cowles refused to cut prices to meet the competition, and readers in Des Moines paid a considerably higher price — 50 cents a month, or about 12 cents a week, for a daily and Sunday subscription to *The Register and Leader*. Subscribers outside Des Moines paid 17 cents a week, or $6 a year by mail, $4 for the daily and $2 for the Sunday paper. Cowles operated on the then current advertising theory that "the higher the price at which a publication is sold, the more the publication is worth . . . to the advertiser" and the longer the publication would be preserved.

Cowles also faced up to the difficult task of collecting unpaid subscription bills, deciding he had to change the system to avoid endless collection problems. In 1908, he ordered subscriptions taken only on a cash-in-advance basis — and the new system worked. Some newspaper businessmen believed that decision would ruin *The Register and Leader,* and one source said circulation did fall "alarmingly" for a time, but average annual figures for the period show an upward trend rather than a collapse.

Another fundamental change that helped the paper was Cowles's decision to use carrier boys to deliver the Sunday paper in cities and towns outside Des Moines that previously could not receive the Sunday edition because postmen did not deliver mail on Sunday. The delivery system outside the city operated through the postal system. Cowles insisted that the carriers give good service, and the carrier commission system turned the boys into salesmen as well as carriers. The more subscribers a carrier recruited, the more profit he made.

Another innovation — having the carriers collect the

advance payments weekly, which meant smaller amounts for a subscriber to have to have on hand — helped keep circulation up.

Advertising as well as circulation problems attracted Cowles's attention early in his publishing reign. He was appalled by full-page ads for trusses, by laxative and cure-all ads, by pitches for products like "Dr. Roe's Silver Medical Discovery," which its purveyors said cured "obstinate coughs, weak and bleeding lungs [and] emaciation." Beer and liquor ads were anathema, too. Cowles and Ingham, both non-drinkers, opposed not only the ads but beer and liquor as well. But, since almost a third of the paper's total display advertising in the early Cowles-Ingham years consisted of "lurid medical nostrums or liquor ads," Cowles had to build circulation strength before he could afford to be selective about the ads *The Register and Leader* accepted. "We need," he said, "to get more circulation to get more advertising to get more money to make a better newspaper to get more circulation."

Some liquor advertising was barred even before a general ban could be instituted. Cowles's son John tells an anecdote that illustrates his father's consistent resistance to advertiser pressure. During an early city election covered by *The Register and Leader*, one of the issues was a drive to cut back closing hours at the city's saloons. *The Register and Leader* advocated the earlier closing hours and said so. With that, representatives of the city's liquor interests came to Gardner Cowles's office and announced that unless the paper changed its editorial policy they were going to withdraw all of their quite-substantial advertising. Without hesitation, John Cowles said, his father declared that the liquor interests certainly were not going to withdraw their advertising — he was canceling it as of that day.

By the end of 1908, circulation had risen to more than 31,000. On the first day of 1909, Cowles announced a total liquor-ad ban. The paper henceforth would refuse "to enter into contracts to print liquor or questionable medical advertising," he said. Iowa's potent "dry" forces hailed the move, and advertising linage grew despite the elimination of the alcohol ads.

Printers, pressmen and other *Register and Leader* employees who drank heavily learned the hard way, some of them, that drinking during working hours was forbidden.

Cowles frequently came unannounced into the newspaper building on Saturday nights, wearing formal dress, either before or after attending a social function, and if he caught employees who had been tippling, they lost their jobs.

On New Year's Eve in 1912, Cowles happened upon a major crisis in the *Register and Leader* composing room, where the paper was being put together mechanically. Cowles, dressed for a party, walked in and looked at the first edition of the Jan. 1, 1913, *Register and Leader* fresh off the press. The paper carried a big promotion advertisement headed "Capturing All Honors," and declaring that *The Register and Leader* carried the largest amount of paid advertising in 1912 of any Des Moines paper. All the city's papers were listed, followed by the traditional 000,000 ciphers used before publication when exact figures are not immediately available. The actual figures had not been inserted and so the comparison table in the few papers that had already rolled off the press showed all of the papers with 000,000 circulation. When the composing room foreman returned, intoxicated, from celebrating the new year, the furious Cowles fired him forthwith.

Other printers meanwhile inserted the correct figures in time for the shipment of several thousand papers headed for northeast Iowa via the Great Western Railroad.

Though he fired liquored-up employees, Cowles always kept on good terms with the printers' union and the other unions as well, recognizing their right to organize. Never during his active management of the paper did he have to cope with a strike, and in 1920, the pressmen's union elected him an honorary member.

Teetotaler Cowles refused "gifts" of liquor steadfastly. Said eldest son Russell Cowles: "In the old days, distillers and brewers left cases of whisky and beer on our back porch during the Christmas season. . . . Father insisted on the stuff being taken away immediately."

In later years, sons John and Mike Cowles wanted the papers to start taking liquor advertising. So they placed clippings of liquor ads from other papers on their father's desk. Gardner Cowles told a secretary: "You needn't bring those ads to me any more. Tell the boys that I throw such ads in the wastebasket." It was not until 1970 and 1971 that the Des Moines Cowles papers resumed taking advertisements for alcoholic beverages — first beer, then liquor.

In 1908, technological advances generated more advertising as luxuries turned into necessities — telephones, electric lights, automobiles were among the advertised goods that boosted linage.

A 1905 report showed *The Register and Leader* wasn't doing badly in competition for column-inches of advertising:

	Local Advertising	Total Advertising
Register and Leader	109,972	244,985
Capital	124,060	237,172
News	127,837	256,604

The Capital did not publish a Sunday paper, and therefore was carrying almost as much advertising in six papers a week as *The Register and Leader* did in seven days. Cowles decided he had to publish an afternoon paper if he wanted to get in on the heaviest allocations of local advertising and if he wanted to make profitable use of his printing plant, which stood idle much of the day after the morning paper was printed overnight.

Across the Des Moines River, on the city's East Side, a contentious editor, one Charles Hellen, had founded *The Des Moines Tribune* as a local Republican daily. Hellen enjoyed firing potshots at assorted targets every day and usually aimed a shot or two at the three West Side papers. When *The Capital* carried a long, colorful story on the demise of beautiful 32-year-old Allie Williams, Des Moines' most famous bawdy house madam, Hellen's *Tribune* raged: "The *Daily Capital* should be spurned by every respectable family in the City of Des Moines as a despoiler of the purity of the home and a menace to the public dignity of the people."

One of *The Tribune's* other complaints was that nobody took it seriously — which was true. When Hellen found he couldn't promote appreciable amounts of advertising from the big West Side advertisers, he sold out in 1908 to owners who turned the paper into a Democratic daily, which ardently supported the 1908 Democratic ticket.

The Republicans swept to victory and *The Tribune* was in tatters. Gardner Cowles bought what was left of the paper on Dec. 1, 1908. John Cowles believes his father paid less than $30,000 for the paper, which had a circulation variously reported at 2,000 to 10,000. Along with the afternoon paper he wanted, Cowles also gained an Associated Press afternoon franchise as well, of considerable importance to his operation's news coverage.

Assorted circulation skirmishes, battles and wars broke out, and *The Tribune* took on the competition with bigger headlines and flashier features than the more sedate morning *Register and Leader. The Tribune* started a daily magazine section with reading aimed at women, with pieces titled "Must a Woman Obey the Man She Marries?", "The Meditations of a Married Man," "The Journal of the Neglected Baby," and a story on each of "50 Famous Indians."

Contrary to his approach on the morning paper, Cowles kept the price on the afternoon *Tribune* low — a penny a paper, or 25 cents a month delivered at home.

With a new paper to sell, the Cowles organization almost doubled the number of subscribers in four years. The morning paper circulation totaled 25,175 in 1906; the combined morning-evening figure reached 49,047 in 1910. Since the pre-Cowles *Tribune* had few readers, much of the gain was new business. *The Sunday Register* went up more slowly — from 22,713 in 1906 to 26,681 in 1910.

A 1911 Polk County history by Johnson Brigham said the papers ranked seventeenth among newspapers west of the Mississippi River and declared that *The Register and Leader* and *The Tribune* spent more money on sports coverage than the total spent on the entire news service of the old *Iowa State Register* in the 1890s.

The history ticked off some figures: "The *Register and Leader* and *Tribune* now receive double leased-wire service of the Associated Press, the same as that received by St. Louis, Minneapolis and St. Paul. It has 35 people on its news and editorial staff, a corps of 20 reporters and about 300 paid correspondents in the field. It has a $38,000 press with the capacity to print 72,000 48-page papers in an hour." Only 21 years before, *The Register* employed a staff of five persons to write and edit the news and editorials.

The papers by the end of 1912 were indeed doing well. The New Year's eve incident of the 000,000 ciphers showed how well. That corrected promotion ad on Jan. 1, 1913 showed that *The Register and Leader* led in total advertising linage and *The Tribune* had made the greatest ad-linage gains over 1911. The list showed that *The Register and Leader* in 1912 had carried 365,372 column inches of advertising, *The Capital* 338,803, *The Tribune* 316,023 and *The News* 260,898.

In later years, Gardner Cowles voiced one regret: He wished that he had renamed the afternoon paper the *Leader* and thereby perpetuated that name in Des Moines newspapering. The *Leader* name was dropped from the morning paper's logotype in 1916.

4 EXPANDING HORIZONS

Harvey Ingham's broad, tolerant editorial attitude remains a force at *The Register* more than a quarter of a century after his death. His capacity for growth through his editorial career became the key to the imprint he left upon the newspaper community's approach to daily journalism, just as Gardner Cowles's attention to detail and his contact with all phases of the in-house operation created a stable environment in which Ingham's expansive approach could thrive.

Always a self-reliant individualist, Ingham had compassion and serenity to spare for others, despite a lifelong digestive ailment that might have turned other men socially as well as physically dyspeptic. Journalist-historian Cyrenus Cole said of him: "I tried to quarrel with Harvey Ingham but he would not quarrel with me, nor with any envious Iowa editor. He smiled and continued to go his own way. He . . . must have possessed some kind of genius. I still cannot make out what kind it was. It may have been the equivalent of the perseverance of saints."

He was admired for his "lucid, piercing editorial style" and his ready wit and "lively sense of humor."

His digestive complaint, which might have been diverticulitis, caused him severe pains periodically — especially on important occasions. On the day in 1894 when the 36-year-old editor married 23-year-old Nellie Hepburn of Des Moines, Ingham had barely said "I do" before he had to dash away to cope with his nervous stomach. The same problem afflicted him at tense political conventions.

He counteracted some of his problem by taking long walks, which did double duty, since he did much of his editorial musing then. "He would walk mile after mile in solemn concentration," one observer said, and "he often passed members of his own family . . . without recognizing them."

His carriage was erect, his hair was white most of his adult life, and he had such good eyes that he could read without glasses into his late 80s. Somewhat above middle height and slightly pudgy at 180 pounds, he was shaped a bit like the popular image of Benjamin Franklin. He regarded his digestive problem with public lightheartedness, once commenting that "when a man's stomach and certain other anatomical functions cease to operate, that man usually turns reformer." He lived to be nearly 91 and in old age was fond of the familiar observation that the way to longevity is to "acquire some sort of ailment in your youth and then take care of yourself the rest of your life."

Newspapering was the key to Ingham's life. The characteristic view of him was that he lived for his work and his family. Until shortly before his death, he went regularly to an office held open for him in the editorial department in the fourth-floor *Register* newsroom.

He wrote 10,000 to 15,000 editorials during his four decades of activity in Des Moines — meeting issues with a code spelled out in an editorial in the style and vintage of 1915:

"Two avenues of popularity are open to the newspaper. The first is to yield, to flatter, to cajole. The second is to stand for the right things unflinchingly and win respect. . . . A strong and fearless newspaper will have readers and a newspaper that has readers will have advertisements. That is the only newspaper formula worth working to. . . . After making all allowances, the only newspaper popularity that counts in the long run is bottomed on public respect."

From the first, Ingham had plenty of opportunity to demonstrate his fortitude in Des Moines — he found himself engulfed in a raging battle between the Standpatters and the Progressives for control of the Iowa Republican Party. He soon made clear that he approved of the Progressive administration of Republican Gov. Albert B. Cummins. Ingham officially switched from his Standpatter allegiance in 1908, but before that he enraged the conservative faction by opposing the free passes that the railroads issued and by favoring the selection of party nominees in primary elections rather than by convention.

For decades, the railroads had dominated Iowa politics, partly by distributing the valuable free passes to state officials and candidates, legislators, party leaders and newspapermen. Because rails were *the* mode of travel, anyone who accepted a pass and its financial benefits found at least some difficulty in fighting the railroads in politics, in the Legislature, or in the newspapers.

In the early 1900s, the Legislature, prodded by Governor Cummins and by Ingham and other editors, outlawed the passes. Ingham had blasted away at the railroads, hinting that if they failed to yield, they faced a dangerously cheap maximum fare. "Unless the railroads of Iowa take themselves out of the field of state politics and begin to attend to the business of railroading strictly," he wrote, "it will not be long before a two-cent [per mile] fare will be forced on them willy-nilly."

The railroads also exercised great power in the party conventions that nominated candidates for state and congressional offices, conventions that contained large blocs of delegates beholden to the railroads. Governor Cummins smashed that setup in 1906 by forcing the adoption of the primary system to choose party nominees. Ingham followed his lead with an editorial that spelled out the argument: "It is just as essential that the people shall nominate the men who are to hold office as it is that they shall elect them. There is only one thing to do and that is to adopt the primary in thoroughgoing fashion and let the people make the nominations."

Such Progressive Republican triumphs did not wipe out the power of the Standpatters, who defeated Cummins for U.S. senator in 1908, although he won a second race for the office a few months later. The Standpatters elected their man, B. F. Carroll, to the governorship the same year.

On economic issues, *The Register* spelled out a strong position in 1910 in favor of careful regulation of big business: "It is not so much an object with people now to prevent big business as it is to have big business done under such supervision as will insure fair play and a reasonable division of the benefits." As for the federal income tax, which went into effect in 1913, the Cowles papers long had supported it as an equitable way of raising federal revenue.

In national politics in the same era, Theodore Roosevelt gave way to William Howard Taft as his Republican successor in the White House in 1909, but Roosevelt disliked the Taft administration so much that in 1912 rumors spread around the country that he would try to seize the presidential nomination from Taft. Ingham's *Register and Leader* editorials were so positive in the belief that Roosevelt would not run that the historian wonders whether Harvey Ingham received such assurance personally from the former president, whom Ingham had called "a believer in a nation that exalts righteousness." When Roosevelt left the White House in 1909, Ingham said of his curbing of big business: "American business will never be conducted on so low a plane as it was before he swung his club or the 'Square Deal.'"

In 1912, Ingham saw in the Taft-Roosevelt rift an opportunity to promote then-Senator Albert B. Cummins as a compromise candidate, but the Iowa GOP spurned that advice and the still-potent Standpatters forced a split delegation, 16 for Taft and 10 for Cummins. With Taft forces in control of the Chicago national convention, Roosevelt bolted and launched the Progressive Party with himself as presidential nominee. The election resulted in the national victory of Democrat Woodrow Wilson and the first post-Civil War triumph for a Democratic presidential nominee in Iowa. At the state level, George W. Clarke, Republican nominee for governor, slipped into office by a margin of fewer than 1,700 votes.

Cummins at one point apparently thought he had had a good chance at the Republican presidential nomination. In a previously unpublished letter to Ingham, Cummins wrote: "After [Roosevelt] knew that there was no possibility of his nomination, the leaders of the Taft crowd sent at least two communications to him proposing my nomination. The first was on the condition that he should withdraw, that Taft would be dropped and that I should be nominated. He declined this proposition. The second communication was that I would be nominated if he would agree not to bolt and to release his delegates, if they desired to be released.

"I do not attempt to give the exact phraseology in which the propositions were submitted to Colonel Roosevelt, but I know they were submitted, and submitted to him personally. I know that in addition to conveying these suggestions, the man who carried them [said] I would not accept the nomination unless I got a majority of the delegates whose titles to their seats were admittedly valid and free from taint. Roosevelt preferred the nomination of Taft and a bolt rather than see a Progressive nominated under the circumstances I have named."

As Ingham's breadth of vision expanded while he grew into his Des Moines editorship, he consistently opposed war. When World War I began in 1914, he continued to urge disarmament: "If ... the United States shall stand, without flinching, for disarmament, the United States can, without any question, dominate the policy of the world.... Now is not the time to be talking about arming America." In 1915, he was indulging in wishful thinking when he wrote: "War will not be tolerated by civilized nations.... This war, as no other war, is writing the condemnation of all war in letters deep and black." Like others before and after him, he could not understand distinctions about which methods of killing in war were "humane" and which were not. "The real crime is warfare in any guise with any kind of implements," he wrote.

In 1916, Ingham and his paper backed the Republican presidential nominee, Charles Evans Hughes, as being "just as likely to keep us out of war as Wilson." Republican Ingham also accused the incumbent Democratic president, Woodrow Wilson, of "shifting opportunism" as the president campaigned on the slogan "He kept us out of war."

When the United States on Apr. 6, 1917 joined the Allied war against Imperial Germany, Ingham saw no other way for the United States but to attempt to seize victory. "The time for internationalism has come," he said, "and the U.S. might as well recognize now as later that our fortunes are tied up with the fortunes of the other democracies of the world. We must join with them for disarmament and for the elimination of war."

Another editorial said: "The judgment of America is definitely against Germany and we shall do what is in the end necessary to make our weight count in the balance." News and photographs of soldiers in war and in training, of bloody fighting and terrible destruction in Europe, of a world-wide food shortage and of the subsequent uneasy peace monopolized newspaper columns for the next few years.

In 1917, *The Register*'s news side was reporting on Iowa-born Herbert Hoover's difficult job of getting food to starving human beings in war-torn Europe and on his direction of global efforts to increase food production and decrease waste. The paper said: "In the past three years, Mr. Hoover has purchased food, clothing and other supplies, but principally food, to the value of $200 million. He has been the sole purchasing and distributing agent for approximately 15 million people and has had to get the food in the world's markets and transport it across a very-much-troubled ocean and through a much-troubled land before it reached the ultimate consumer."

As the war intensified in mid-1917, the food situation worsened. In a letter printed in *The Register* and elsewhere, Hoover said that "the world's stock of food has reached a point lower than was ever known before in modern times." Grocery stores in the United States limited sales of sugar to half a pound per customer, housewives who bought flour to bake bread had to take some of it as corn meal, and families were asked to observe "meatless Tuesdays" and "wheatless Wednesdays."

Elsewhere on the home front, fervent Iowa patriots persecuted their "German" neighbors after the United States declared war. A mob put a rope around a German's neck at Titonka because he "would not buy enough war bonds," and zealots slapped coats of yellow paint on the homes of persons of German origin. In Kossuth County, the town of Germania changed its name to Lakota, and Berlin, in Tama County, became Lincoln.

Harvey Ingham attacked the attackers, declaring that "the utmost confidence prevails here in Iowa" in the loyalty of persons of German origin. He defended German literature and objected to halting the teaching of German in the public schools shortly before the country entered the war, writing: "We are coming into a new and much larger world and, instead of cutting off our knowledge of languages and literature of the world, we should enlarge it."

In 1918, with the war in its last bitter stages, Governor William L. Harding issued a proclamation against the use of foreign languages in Iowa schools and elsewhere, including telephone conversations. Some zealots reportedly whistled into phones and broke up conversations on country lines in Dutch-speaking neighborhoods of northwest Iowa. Ingham was not much opposed to discouraging the use of German in conversations, he said, "but to stop the speaking of French or Bohemian or Yiddish or any of the Scandinavian languages would be not only an unfriendly act to some of the best Americans we have but would be essentially un-American." The governor's proclamation was all but unenforceable; too many Iowans used the languages of their mother countries.

Ingham's support of Woodrow Wilson withstood severe testing when the Democratic president, fearing that a Republican legislative majority might thwart his world peace plans, asked American voters to elect a Democratic

Congress in 1918. When Republicans reacted angrily against Wilson, Ingham wrote an editorial entitled "Stand By the President." It read: "The President has his limitations and they are very marked, but he has great talent and it is a talent particularly suited to the times. With the possible exception of Lincoln, America has never had a man who could say so much to help the cause of free government in the world, and so little to hurt it, as President Wilson . . . .

"The opportunity is here for America to dominate the future. The President has proposed a program that has brought hope to every oppressed people. With astonishing unanimity Europe has consented to the broad outlines of reorganization. Why can not America consent to recognize that we must win or lose in the two years the President has yet to serve, leaving the incidental irritations of Democratic control at Washington out of it, concentrate on the great world triumph we can win if we possess a united front."

The *Register*'s views flew in the face of the stereotype of the Midwest as the bastion of isolationist Republican opinion unsullied by critical judgment. After the voters rejected Wilson's appeal and elected a Republican Congress in November, 1918, and after the armistice was signed Nov. 11, *The Register* again urged the nation to seize the opportunity for lasting peace. Ingham wrote: "*The Register* believes the President should be given the benefit of the doubt and that for the time being partisan opposition should be wholly dropped."

For a year after the war's end, President Wilson and his opponents continued struggling over the proposed League of Nations. The President toured the country trying to whip up public sentiment for approval of a peace treaty that included creation of the League. On Sept. 6, 1919, Wilson spoke in the old Des Moines Coliseum, demanding that Congress accept the proposals without change and declaring that the League "secures peace in the only way peace can be secured." Downtown, 70,000 people jammed the streets during the Wilson visit.

Ingham poured out his heart in a series of editorials imploring the country and its leaders to follow Wilson's lead. "What will the next war cost America?" Ingham asked. "Would anybody face that alternative and then worry over the incidental burdens and expenses of world organizations? . . . The cheapest money the American taxpayer ever will be called upon to pay will be the money needed to provide an international tribunal for the world .... The wisest nationalism the American citizen ever will show will be the nationalism that is international."

Having written many editorials backing Wilson, Ingham once explained his unusual political posture this way: "It is a good time to cast every political consideration aside, every prejudice, and to reflect how marvelously fortunate this republic has been in the leadership of Woodrow Wilson at this part of its existence." Another time, he wrote in his internationalist vein: "It will be to the everlasting glory of America that in time of world babble, the American voice was heard above them all ... in ringing tones of assurance of a better world, a more livable world, a more humane world."

When the wording of the League convenant was made public, Ingham praised its "sober practicality, its courage ... its strict adherence to the purpose of abolishing war." He added: "The League is not an end but a beginning. It is a great moment in history." But he was disappointed in the covenant's "failure in definite terms to commit the world to disarmament."

Ingham also took issue with Wilson on the President's refusal to agree to a Japanese plea to include a racial-equality clause in the covenant. Consistent in his support of minority races, he declared that Asians "have precisely the same rights as Caucasians." He said: "There should be nothing in this new period we are entering to suggest race superiority or inferiority. Why then should politics tolerate the notion when it is so fraught with possibilities of trouble?"

Despite Wilson's efforts and the campaigns of editors like Ingham, the Senate late in 1919 turned down the League treaty. Disgusted with Congress's performance, Ingham said in a letter to his son William: "I never saw such petty bickering in the face of a crisis as is going on in Washington. It is a disgrace to the whole people. Not one man in Congress is saying anything worth listening to, much less worth preserving."

Harvey Ingham never retreated from his insistence that mankind had to set up some sort of strong international organization. The formation of the United Nations after World War II made at least some of Ingham's and others' unsuccessful campaigns worth the effort.

Ingham over the years also feared military domination

of American life and objected to compulsory military training. "In what way will the U.S. be an improvement over Germany if we are to have compulsory conscription of high school and college students for training to think in terms of 'success in battle'?" he asked. Consistent to the core, he required commitment on issues like this one. After a 1926 Presbyterian church assembly dodged the issue, he criticized churchmen for not opposing military training. *The Register* then asked: "Just what is the scope of the church? Shall it be limited to preaching righteousness in vague generalities and have nothing to say about it in a specific way?"

In 1919, *The Register* and *The Tribune* fought hard for two other fundamental issues facing the people besides the League of Nations cause. Women's suffrage and Prohibition received strong *Register* and *Tribune* support.

Naively expecting the ban on manufacturing and selling liquor to prove effective, the papers supported Prohibition of liquor and beer. As early as 1917, before Prohibition, *The Register* said editorially: "It is a safe venture that when United States officers have made a few enforcement arrests, liquor for beverage purposes will be practically unknown in this state." After the Eighteenth Amendment to the U.S. Constitution went into effect in 1920, prohibiting the manufacture, sale and transportation of intoxicating liquors in the United States, the murderous bootleg era began. Enforcement failed generally. In 1933, most of the nation was glad to repeal the Prohibition amendment.

In 1917, Ingham had called liquor a greater cause of "poverty, idleness, crime, disease and general cussedness" than any other. *The Register* credited the high productivity of workers largely to Prohibition. "In the end," an editorial said, "no European industry will be able to compete on even terms if the anti-liquor movement does not reach European labor." Despite strenuous efforts of "dry" leaders like Ingham, Iowans in a referendum voted 3-to-2 in favor of the Twenty-First Amendment, which ultimately repealed the Prohibition Amendment.

More satisfactory was the experience with women's suffrage. The certification in 1920 of the ratification of the Nineteenth Amendment, granting voting rights to women in all states, was a notable victory for campaigners like Ingham.

Human rights were always an Ingham cause. He never backed down from his strong support for equal rights for people of color as well as for women. He objected to the Immigration Act of 1924, which established an annual national-origins quota of immigrants to the United States that (until 1968) discriminated in favor of immigrants from the countries of northwestern Europe and against those from Asian and southeast European countries. In one instance, he called U.S. policy an insult to the Japanese and said the law, a virtual ban on Japanese immigration, was based on an "underlying feeling of race." He commented: "It will help everybody to come to correct conclusions about a lot of social and political problems if they will get in mind once for all that the races of men are of one original stock. . . . There is nothing in the theory of superior races and superior classes. Nature has a way of her own of keeping the earth a melting pot and genius still springs from the most unexpected sources."

During the early years of World War I, Ingham became a member of the Des Moines chapter of the National Association for the Advancement of Colored People (NAACP) and in the 1920s thrust himself into the middle of the unsettling resurgence of the Ku Klux Klan (KKK). He wanted no part of the anti-black, anti-Semitic, anti-Catholic, anti-foreign organization of men in white robes and peaked hats, and said so. But during the Twenties, the Klan — open only to white, non-Jewish, non-Catholic and native-born citizens — became a formidable force in the nation, in Iowa and in Des Moines. In 1923, the white supremacist organization reportedly had 2,500 members in Des Moines and was said to be signing up 200 recruits a week. Half the police officers in the city and a couple of school board members reportedly were Klansmen, and a city councilman riding a white horse led a Klan parade through downtown Des Moines.

In 1926, an estimated 20,000 Iowa Klansmen gathered in Des Moines for a meeting and in one night 12 fiery crosses, symbol of Klan presence, burned in the city. On another night, news reports told of "scores" of crosses — too many to count — burning all over town, including one on the lawn of a black family that had moved into a white neighborhood.

Ingham condemned both the racism and the way Klansmen made threats against citizens who had done things that Klansmen thought were contrary to the mores of the times. "The man who does not know that the races are all here and are all going to be here, and [that] until their common rights are recognized there can be no peace and security for anyone, is not yet out of the international kindergarten," he wrote. He attacked the exercise of such "justice" by the Klan by comparing it with the methods of pioneer vigilantes who hanged without trial men suspected of being horse thieves. "History makes it plain as daylight," Ingham said, "that no society can be either safe or sound where justice is not administered in the orderly manner of public tribunal."

He paid close attention to the progress of blacks, writing in 1933 that since Negroes "who are already in the front rank of music and art are the products of only two generations since the Civil War, there is one conclusion to be drawn, and that is that the Negro is going to compete on even terms everywhere within the time of the boys and girls now crowding the public schools."

His concern for American Indian rights was as strong as that for other minorities; the man who as a boy hid with his mother from the threat of Indian attackers was in his adulthood to admire and defend Indian customs. He subscribed to the Indian theory that a male child should not be subjected to the indignity of spanking. He used this approach with his three sons, Hepburn, William and Harvey, jr., who not only remembered the lack of spanking but also recalled being held on their father's knee while he read to them, from Shakespeare, from "Ivanhoe" and "The Pilgrim's Progress." They remembered, too, the breakfast-table contest to see who could memorize the most sayings of Poor Richard for a 10-cent prize.

Ingham's long and deeply felt concern for the underprivileged was apparent as early as a 1905 *Register and Leader* picture story on Des Moines housing that ran under his aegis. The story accompanying a picture of a rundown dwelling asked: "Can we blame a man or a woman compelled to live in [such] a house if he drinks and is not all he should be? Can we blame the children reared under these conditions if they do not grow up into good upright men and women? Is it not our duty as citizens of this great and good republic to work for better citizens and therefore for better conditions? ..." A quarter of a century later, in the 1930s Depression, he continued to express concern about underprivileged children and to insist that the "self-reliant" among the citizenry must assume responsibility for individuals who cannot solve their own problems.

In a radio talk on the problems of welfare and the children of welfare families, he declared that fully half the children in Des Moines were "living under conditions not stimulating in health and vigor." Long before the establishment of governmental aid to dependent children, he said, in his Nineteenth Century style: "Every child in Iowa and in Des Moines should be well-born, and should enjoy in its first five years sanitary food in a sanitary home."

Combining his usual common sense with his equally characteristic compassion in dealing with human problems, he said the "essential habits of life" are formed in a child's first five years. He pointed to the danger of children "growing up into a deep-seated hostility to their social surroundings" and he warned that someday such persons might "number enough in a period of distress to overturn the established social order."

In addition to his anti-war, temperance, equal-rights and aid-to-the-hungry causes, Ingham also campaigned over the years for full employment and a "fair" income for the farmer. He clung tenaciously to some of his positions even though they failed and he backed some horses that didn't cross the wire at all.

In 1928, *The Register* declared: "We are in a new era. National prosperity is going to last." The Great Depression began the next year.

Another earlier depression gave birth to one of Ingham's long-run campaigns for an unsuccessful cause. In a six-month-long collapse of farm prices in 1920, the price of corn dropped to 67 cents a bushel from $1.75 and hog prices fell at an alarming rate as post-World War I foreign markets all but disappeared. Effects of the disastrous slump ricochetted through the economy — and Ingham felt that at least part of the trouble could have been avoided if the United States had embarked on a substantial program of foreign aid. Help war-devastated economies resume industry so they can produce goods to exchange for American products and you automatically aid U.S. sellers, he said, driving the point home: "Nobody knows how much we must suffer in our own purses before we learn that the commercial world is one, and that leaving any part of it in bankruptcy in the end will bankrupt all the rest."

Despite that internationalist stand, he supported a tarriff proposal called the McNary-Haugen bill, sponsored in Congress by U.S. Senator Charles McNary of Oregon and Representative Gilbert Haugen of Northwood, Iowa. The proposal basically was an export plan that would permit U.S. farmers to receive higher prices for surpluses sold overseas than the prevailing world market would permit. In return, farmers would pay an "equalization fee" to cover any losses by the U.S. government in helping operate the export subsidy plan. In general, this meant a two-price system for farmers — an export, or subsidized, price, and a domestic price — for their major commodities.

Ingham argued that if tariffs protected American industry they also should protect farm income. President Calvin Coolidge vetoed the proposal twice, in 1927 and 1928, arguing that it would result in a "clamor" for more subsidies for other industries and that it would spawn new surpluses.

During his term in office, President Hoover did not support McNary-Haugen, but he did in 1929 sponsor the Agricultural Marketing Act, which created a federal farm board to which Congress appropriated $500 million to strengthen prices by permitting the board to buy up cotton and wheat surpluses. A *Register* editorial gave Hoover credit for "giving the farmer a working organization," but for some years, although the board spent all of its money buying surpluses, the purchases failed to help farm prices. The board also urged farmers to cut their plantings, recommending a 30 per cent cut in wheat acreage, for example, but it had no power to pay individual farmers for reducing acreage. That is what President Franklin D. Roosevelt's New Deal farm program began doing in 1933. Droughts in 1934 and 1936, which cut farm production one-third, helped prices rise at the same time the program went into effect.

Rejection of the McNary-Haugen principle by two successive GOP presidents was one of the factors that helped pave the way for Democratic victories in Iowa in the 1932, 1934 and 1936 elections. Ingham consistently supported the principle of federal assistance to agriculture, backing the extensive farm programs of F.D.R. and Agriculture Secretary Henry A. Wallace even though he remained a Republican. In his old age, Ingham conceded that "it is a little difficult for me to be enthusiastic over government aid [but] I do insist on one thing, and that is that if the government is going to aid anybody, it should aid the farmer first."

In his personal life, Ingham relied on the efficacy of laughter, which he called "the measure of man's superiority," to meet the psychological defeats of the Depression and the shadow of World War II. He also possessed a strong philosophical vein and a belief in the power of religion.

Shortly before he moved to Des Moines, he contemplated the usefulness of contemplation itself, making a case for observing the sabbath. He wrote: "Some time must be set apart for the serious consideration of the higher things of life. Man occupies some relationship ... to that power in the world which makes for righteousness. Neither his business occupation nor his amusements train him in all that is required of him as a responsible human being." Declaring that it is easy to ridicule Puritanism, he was sure that the "stern faith and rigid convictions" of America's founders were essential to America's "accomplishment of great and noble things."

5 THE COWLES STYLE

From the beginning, Gardner Cowles expected as much of himself as of his employees. He went to his office by streetcar, usually before 7 a.m., and ended his working day about 6 p.m. He was not an easy man to work for and did not hesitate to crack the whip if he thought someone needed it.

Cowles was a difficult boss, one newspaper official said, "in the sense that there were no alternatives with him. You were to get certain things done, period. You did not talk about excuses or problems. It was just a matter of getting it done. He immediately set a new goal once the old goal was reached." He simply wanted a full day's work out of each employee. Many years after Cowles's death, a longtime employee said: "If Gardner Cowles had not been cremated, he would be spinning in his grave over the coffee breaks that the employees take each day. He wouldn't have stood for them in his day."

Occasionally, Harvey Ingham would drink coffee with workers in the Bluebird, a small restaurant-cafe in the old Register and Tribune Building. When one staff member asked Cowles: "Why don't you stop and have coffee with us?" Cowles said he didn't have the time. The employee said: "Harvey joins us for coffee; he has the time." With the bare flicker of a smile, Cowles retorted: "Harvey doesn't have the money I have."

City circulation manager Sam Miller also got the don't-waste-time treatment when one day he announced an unusual situation: Every newsboy in the city had turned in his collection money on time and Miller didn't have to go out on a collection tour with the boys. "That's fine," Cowles said. "That will leave you more time to go out after more circulation."

He was happy to delegate authority — where he was certain the results would be good. "If he asked you to do something and he found that you were doing it correctly, that was your job from then on, no matter how much time, how many hours it took," one employee said.

His demanding approach did not blind Cowles to what an employee was worth. The same official stressed that Cowles "treated me well and gave me the encouragement I needed. When I was tempted to leave, he told me he thought there was a good future for me in the newspaper and he encouraged me to stay. I did and never regretted it."

In the public arena, while Harvey Ingham took much of the political heat directed against *Register* stands, Gardner Cowles dealt with another brand of attempted influence. Through his career, Cowles was the target of pressure from advertisers who, in the mistaken belief that payment for advertising buys more than the space in which the ad runs, tried to block publication of news stories.

As early as 1904, Cowles encountered pressure. One of those classic reporter-management cases developed in which a manager's definition of "fairness" sounds to a reporter as if it is advice to pull punches. The case involved a reporter named Don Berry, later a notable Indianola, Iowa editor. While covering a bitter Des Moines school election, Berry tried to be impartial but produced stories in which, he said, "the facts did favor one side more than the other." Someone complained to Cowles and the publisher cautioned Berry to be "very careful" about what he wrote because "we had subscribers and advertisers in both camps and we had to be careful not to offend them." The warning disturbed Berry, who did not learn until later that Cowles was concentrating his attention on his difficult financial situation.

Trying to cope with his problem, Berry went to Editor Ingham for advice on how to handle the stories. Ingham shot back: "Write the truth and let the chips fall where they may." Declaring that that was what he had been doing, Berry continued his coverage as before. He heard no more from Cowles and later commented: "Let it not be assumed from that incident that Gardner Cowles lacked courage." On another subject, as a matter of policy, Cowles and Ingham always refused readers' pleas to kill stories about arrests on drunken-driving charges.

Reminiscing in 1941, Cowles looked back to 1903 and the early years: "In the beginning," he said, "the paper was little, very little in terms of readers, of employees, of equipment, of property, of the services it was able to give. It was little and weak — so weak that often, in some years, its very survival seemed uncertain."

In 1919, long after he was well established in Des Moines, Cowles clashed with a major advertiser, A. H. Blank, a longtime Iowa motion picture power. Proud of the new Iowa Building he had had constructed in downtown Des Moines, Blank arranged the dedication day with particular care and expected the story to be carried on Page One of *The Register*. But his timing was bad. President Wilson returned that day to New York City from his historic League of Nations peace mission in Europe and the story monopolized Page One.

The angry Blank, his dedication story relegated to an inside page, canceled his theater advertising — an action that involved considerable sums of money. Cowles took it coolly. "Don't worry," he said, "we can get along better without him than he can without us." Blank soon resumed his advertising.

Some years later reporter Hasson (Bill) Millhaem dug up the story of a divorce action involving the elder Fred Fitch, Des Moines hair tonic manufacturer. Fitch telephoned Millhaem and told him: "You aren't going to print that story. I left an order with your paper for 16 pages of hair tonic and shampoo advertising. You aren't going to kick all that business out the window. Come on out and play golf."

Instead, Millhaem wrote the story, which was printed in full; Fitch canceled the advertising, and Millhaem "never heard a word of complaint from Cowles or anybody else."

Sometimes Cowles did try to ease the impact of a difficult story — and found himself overruled by the news-freedom principles he himself had helped establish. One evening he came to the newsroom after hearing that a relative of an important advertiser had been convicted of a crime and was headed for the penitentiary. "Now, we don't want to keep such a story out of the paper," Cowles told an editor. "I think I would put the story on an inside page and put this kind of a head [a relatively small one] on it."

Forrest Seymour, the editor on duty that night, had planned to carry the story on the next morning's Page One under a banner headline. After Cowles passed the word, Seymour telephoned William W. (Bill) Waymack, then managing editor, and anxiously asked for advice. "Go ahead with the Page One story as you had planned it in the first place. I'll see the old gentleman in the morning," Waymack replied.

The story ran on Page One and Editor Seymour heard no further word about it.

Cowles would not countenance leaving out of the paper a story unfavorable to anyone connected directly or indirectly with his newspapers. After hearing a report on the street that a member of the family of a top *Register* official had been picked up on a driving charge "Mr. Cowles really let me have it because we had not printed the story," said Stuffy Walters, then managing editor. "But we had nothing to go on. There was nothing on the police records. That was as close as I ever came to getting fired." Police officials insisted they had made no such arrest, and no story ever appeared.

In another situation, a distant relative of the Cowles family figured in a University of Iowa investigation in the early 1930s. "We were told to use every last bit of testimony about that relative in the paper, no matter how trivial," said Glen Cunningham, then city editor.

Cowles insisted, as did later generations of the family, that news of the family neither be played down nor suppressed. Thus, the reports of the three divorces of Gardner Cowles, jr., appeared on Page One.

One of the Cowles-Ingham team's bitterest political battles raged during the World War I years in a conflict with William L. Harding, a leading Sioux City Republican who was elected lieutenant governor in 1912 and re-elected in 1914 despite the opposition of Cowles and Ingham. They charged he was supported by special interests, including "saloon interests."

The dispute had its roots partly in Lieutenant Governor Harding's presumed blocking of a six-year appointment of Gardner Cowles to the governing body that preceded the State Board of Regents as supervisor of state universities and colleges. The Iowa Senate, over which Harding presided, approved Cowles for a short term, which ran until July 1, 1915. The Senate refused, however, to confirm him for a six-year term ending in 1921. Cowles did not even stay on the board until the end of the short term, resigning in April, 1915 after two months' service.

In 1916, William Harding sought the Republican nomination for governor and the Cowles papers opposed him again. The opposition arose not only because of Cowles's defeat but also because Harding favored the sale of liquor in Iowa and because Harding, the "mud road candidate," opposed paving Iowa's main roads. With his customary foresight, Cowles was focusing on the growing possibilities of motor traffic, and his newspapers launched an intensive campaign favoring "hard roads." (In 1910, Iowa registered 10,000 motor vehicles; in 1920, the state's annual registration exceeded 400,000.)

The Cowles-Harding conflict climaxed shortly before the June 6, 1916 primary election, when Harding published an advertisement around the state declaring that Cowles had offered in 1915 to support Harding for governor in 1916 in return for Harding's help in getting confirmation to the college-governing board. The ad also said that Harry Watts, the Cowles papers' advertising manager, tried to sell Harding political advertising even while the papers were saying that liquor money helped finance the Harding campaign.

The ad enraged the normally mild-mannered Cowles. *The Register* replied with a rare Page One statement by Cowles and a scathing Jay Darling cartoon picturing Harding as a frog sitting in a mud puddle labeled "Iowa roads" and croaking "Jug-o'-rum! Jug-o'-rum!" Cowles's statement, under the headline "Unfit," said:

"William L. Harding's statement that I offered to support him in exchange for confirmation is a lie, unqualified by the slightest word, act, intimation or suggestion on my part.

"Further statements by him in advertisements which appeared in a number of papers last evening, purporting to give the words or substance of a conversation between him and Harry Watts are likewise absolutely false. *The Register* has consistently opposed Mr. Harding since his legislative record disclosed his lack of character."

The Register's stand took a beating in the election. Harding easily won the Republican nomination for governor over three opponents. *The Register* also lost its campaign backing an amendment to the Iowa Constitution to give women the right to vote in all elections. The women's suffrage amendment lost by a close margin.

In 1916's fall general election, *The Register* and *The Tribune,* though still identifying themselves as Republican papers, supported Democrat E. T. Meredith for governor against Harding. The latter easily defeated Meredith, an opponent of the sale of liquor and an advocate of paved highways.

Harding tried to make peace with the Cowles papers,

sending an emissary to offer Cowles a state appointment. Cowles told the messenger: "Go back and tell the governor I'm not interested. He knows what I think of him. Tell him that I haven't changed my mind."

The heat had been fierce. Cowles's secretary, the late Agnes MacDonald, remembered putting into Gardner Cowles's mailbox "all the letters saying awful things about him" in his campaign to clean up Republican politics. "Certain people did not like the [reformist] idea," she said. "They threatened to 'get' him, his business and his family. He read all those letters. I don't think they bothered him too much. He did not lose his courage at all."

In the midst of 1916's various political campaigns, Gardner Cowles agreed to be a delegate to the Republican national convention. Albert B. Cummins was Iowa's "favorite son" presidential candidate. Howard Clark, a leading Des Moines lawyer and politician and also a convention delegate, and Mrs. Cowles accompanied Cowles to Chicago.

"The Iowans hired a band," John Cowles recalled. "After the nominating speech, they staged a demonstration for Cummins on the convention floor. My mother said she never saw anything sillier than my father and Clark and the rest of the Iowans parading around the hall wearing silly little hats with 'Cummins for President' on them. They all felt they were damn fools, and they were, but they tried to make the demonstration last as long as they could," which amounted to three or four minutes. The Cummins drive got nowhere, Charles Evans Hughes won the nomination, and incumbent President Woodrow Wilson won a close election.

In 1918, the papers tried hard to defeat Governor Harding's bid for re-election, one editorial declaring: "Nobody who knows the inside workings of the Statehouse during the last two years would put the governor back." *The Register* and other Iowa papers covered two lively scandals involving the governor's office. One concerned a rape pardon-bribery case that spawned unsuccessful impeachment proceedings. The second linked Governor Harding's office with losses suffered by investors who bought stock in a planned Des Moines packinghouse that never was built.

In the 1918 election, Cowles and Ingham supported a highly regarded Democrat, Claude Porter, who gave Harding a scare in the race but lost by a small margin. After leaving office in 1921, Harding remained active in public affairs almost until his death in 1935 but never held office again.

In addition to his political conservatism, Cowles was conservative as well in his financial life. Prudence with money was an essential part of his philosophy — but he never hesitated to spend large amounts of cash if he believed his newspapers would benefit substantially. With the advent of his push for better Iowa roads, but still at a time when employees thought twice about spending extra money, he told a circulation department worker: "I think we ought to spend $50 a day extra to start some motor hauls taking *The Tribune* to towns we're not reaching now." The effort was consistent with Cowles's positive approach, which the circulation employee summed up as: "To advance and enlarge the scope of coverage and service."

Cowles would spend large sums, but that was because he was careful with small amounts. An executive and his secretary once made a one-cent error in adding the payroll and "Cowles really let me have it," the executive said. "It was not the one-cent error, but the principle of the thing. 'If you are that careless on the payroll,' he said, 'how do I know that you won't make a bigger mistake on something else?"

Mathematically skillful, Cowles could look down a column of figures and tell immediately if the total was incorrect. Said John Cowles: "My father, in addition to concentrating on building circulation, scrutinized every penny of operating expense and personally checked and okayed every bill before it was paid and also signed each payroll check himself."

His theory on taking charge of the paper was that paying attention to small items could be the difference between a profitable and a losing operation. On Sundays after the family attended church (initially First Methodist, later other Protestant churches), Cowles would drop in at the Locust Street plant. Henry Wilcots, longtime *Register* custodial employee, described the Cowles inspection tours:

"Mr. Cowles came to the building every Sunday morning after church. He had me take him on the elevator to the thirteenth floor. He carried a pencil and pad and walked all the way down, stopping on each floor on the way. He looked into every office and restroom. If he found a light left on, water running or records spread around on a desk, he left a note. The people in those offices found the notes Monday morning," and presumably mended their ways.

As in most business and professional operations, periodic anti-waste campaigns sprang up. In the 1930s, Managing Editor Stuffy Walters ordered editors and reporters to bring back to the office all the newspaper pencils they had accumulated at home. It is one of the characteristics of reporters and editors that they accumulate clutches of pencils at home, in pockets, in purses, in desk drawers. After Walters took the customary ribbing for his "return-the-pencils" edict, he said he had done it on Cowles's orders.

Cowles's presence kept everyone in the building on the alert. Newcomers were warned on their first day on the job never to say "I don't know" if Cowles asked for information but to promise to get it immediately and then to drop everything and get it. Every local ad sold was recorded in a book in the local-ad department at the head of one flight of stairs. "If you saw Mr. Cowles coming up the stairs," said one employee, "you had better get that book up to date but fast."

Cowles's probity and financial soundness paid off when he needed money. Once, in the early *Register and Leader* years, he sought a $10,000 loan from J. G. Rounds, president of the old Citizens National Bank of Des Moines. He signed the note, got the money and offered to put up collateral. Rounds merely replied: "When we want collateral, we'll let you know."

Stalling or offering alibis irritated Cowles; he insisted on facing up to situations immediately and he wanted everyone in the organization to do the same. His secretary, Agnes MacDonald, had the right temperament for working with Cowles (few secretaries did, he was "too exacting for most women," she said). She recalled once saying to Cowles: "When you're not busy, I'd like to file these letters," and he answered: "Let's do it now." "That was Mr. Cowles," she said, " 'let's do it now.' "

In the early days at least, Cowles insisted that his employees maintain good credit ratings with Des Moines merchants. He checked every new edition of a city credit-rating book to see how well employees were paying their bills. When the book indicated that a major official of the paper was having credit troubles, word came down from Cowles that there was to be no more of that, and the official fell into line.

One of the few battles Cowles did lose with his employees was his effort to ban smoking in the newspaper building. He was a non-smoker.

Cowles did not regard himself as a financial wizard. When someone asked him how he might have fared had he been in Algona during the Depression, he said: "I'd have gone broke, like everyone else."

Despite his cool exterior, he was concerned about his employees' welfare. Sometimes his approach was paternalistic, sometimes empathetic. Once he reprimanded an office girl for doing a job in what he thought was the wrong way. When his secretary pointed out that the girl's procedure was correct and he was wrong, Cowles without a further word walked to the girl's desk and apologized. During the Depression, Cowles took photographer George Yates by the arm in the newspaper building's lobby one day and stood silent for a moment as homeward-bound workers streamed by. "Mr. Yates, I wonder what would happen to these people if I could not make these papers go," he said. Business had declined so badly that he had ordered a 10 per cent pay cut; as soon as the economic situation improved, salaries went up again.

At about the same time, the company's chief attorney, Fred Little, served notice that he wanted to sell his Register and Tribune Company stock because "the country is going over the dam." When Cowles heard that, he bought Little's stock with the comment: "We're going to have some tough times probably, but the country is not going over the dam." In June, 1936, Fred Little repurchased the same number of stock shares he had sold back to the Register and Tribune Company in November, 1935.

Wherever he went, Cowles tried to keep in touch with the office. One summer, when he took the family on a vacation at a ranch 18 miles from Sheridan, Wyo., he arranged for daily business reports to be mailed to him. The mail, however, came to the ranch only once or twice a week. Being out of touch was a situation he couldn't tolerate, so the very first day he borrowed a horse — although he hadn't ridden in several years — and rode into town. Seven hours later he returned on foot, leading the horse that carried the sack of mail. After that case of saddle sores, Cowles paid a cowboy to ride into town for the mail each day.

The mail fascinated him. "I don't think I've ever known anyone who loved the mail so much as Mr. Cowles," said Opal Wilson, a secretary in the Register and Tribune Company's executive offices who began work at the firm in 1917. "I came to work at 7 in the morning," she said. "Mr.

Cowles was already there. He opened letters with his penknife and read and checked all the mail. He once said to me: 'People should not send postcards here because we'll read them, won't we?' and we both did." Cowles didn't think anything of opening and reading letters addressed to his sons, she said: "If the envelope said 'Cowles' on it, he read it. When they were young, the boys asked me to intercept any pink or scented envelopes addressed to them."

To cope with daily pressures, Cowles played duffer golf for a while; he also liked to play bridge, particularly in his later years, but traveling and seeing plays were his favorite pastimes. He enjoyed "doing" a week's worth of plays in New York, and had a habit of returning to plays he especially liked — he saw Eugene O'Neill's "Strange Interlude" three times and George Ade's "The County Chairman" five times.

On Cowles's travels, his methodical approach to life went with him. "Everything had to be on schedule," one of his associates said. "He felt a greater satisfaction in making a close train connection than in seeing the Grand Canyon." Not quite — he not only enjoyed seeing and studying exotic places, but he also liked giving travelogue reports before clubs like the old, prestigious Prairie Club.

Physically, Cowles looked like the conservative businessman he was. He was about 5 foot 9, weighed 175 to 180 pounds and wore spectacles and somber business suits.

Conservative and stern though he often appeared, he could express paradoxically liberal sentiments. Reporter Agnes Arney, who knew him well, once told him that a prominent Des Moines woman had had a child out of wedlock and had left Des Moines. "Mr. Cowles said: 'If a woman wants a baby, there is nothing terribly wrong with her having it, even if she isn't married,' " Mrs. Arney said.

Cowles didn't gamble in the usual sense, but he often bet nickels with veteran *Register* political reporter C. C. (Cy) Clifton on the outcome of city elections. "He followed city politics closely and usually beat me," Clifton said, "and he was a great guy for getting information by asking questions" — a trait the Cowles sons inherited and developed.

Although he concentrated principally on the business end of the papers, Cowles kept close track of the news, reading the papers thoroughly. To hold the trust of its readers, he knew that a paper had to be honest. And to keep its subscribers, he knew that the nurturing of a policy of teamwork would produce an even better newspaper.

Cowles went out of his way frequently to credit employees for the papers' successes. "Co-operation will win in building up a business just as it will in a football game," he said in 1915. "I appreciate what 250 people employed by *The Register and Leader* and *The Tribune* are doing toward increasing both advertising and circulation." (By 1977, the papers employed more than 1,200 persons.)

In 1941, when Cowles was 80, he said: "It is gratifying to me that so many of our 'newspaper family' have shared with me the labor of building through so many of these years. And it *has* been a shared labor. The one greatest asset that this institution has had — the one that I have tried hardest to create and preserve — has been the spirit of teamwork in so marked a degree that we have had."

Discussing the function of newspapers, he declared: "Without good newspapers, I doubt whether any people under modern conditions can preserve free institutions. . . . The good newspaper must be honest. It must be fair. It must be truly efficient in every respect in the job of delivering to a free people with the maximum speed the information by which they alone can manage their common affairs themselves as a self-governing group."

Cowles's distinctive gift was to be able to hew to a conservative cast of thought and yet permit his papers to express a wide divergence of opinion and news coverage. Those were decisive reasons for the acceptance of *The Register* and *The Tribune* even during the Thirties Depression. The freedom that Cowles and Ingham gave competent newsmen was summed up by one veteran editor: "If you have qualified people, you are far better off if you get out of their way and let them function than if you are looking over their shoulders all the time. That's the way Mr. Cowles was with the news department."

Sometimes the results puzzled discerning readers who observed the contradictory viewpoints expressed by staff members.

"I pick up *The Register* in the morning and I see a cartoon by Ding on Page One," an Iowa editor said. "I may find an editorial by Bill Waymack on the editorial page of that same newspaper which disagrees with Ding's position on the front page. Then there may be a column by Harvey Ingham that says something else and there may be a story by C. C. Clifton that does not agree with any of them. I don't see how such a paper operates."

Ward Barnes, publisher of *The Eagle,* a weekly newspaper in Eagle Grove, Iowa, responded to that comment with a perceptive and succinct analysis.

Said Barnes: "I'll explain *The Register* to you. It is very much like the British Empire. *The Register* is made up of a lot of autonomous units with not a lot in common except their allegiance to one family."

Barnes's analysis was based on the Thirties *Register,* but the loyalty to the Cowles-Ingham regime began much earlier and continued much later. In the early days, growth was on everyone's mind at *The Register.*

6 MUD ROADS AND FAILING BANKS

One of Gardner Cowles's cardinal beliefs was that subscribers would keep the reader habit if the circulation crew, from subscription takers through carriers, provided reliable, regular delivery. "A good newspaper promptly delivered can scarcely shake off the subscribers with dynamite," he maintained.

As America's railroads began their long decline, Cowles turned his business eye toward roads and motor delivery as the key to his distribution and circulation plans. Turning one's eyes toward roads in those days was the act of an invincible optimist and believer in the character-building (and, perhaps, profit-making) virtues of taking on an uphill battle.

For generations, mud roads had blighted traffic in Iowa. When heavy rains fell, when snow melted or when frost left the ground, drivers had to wrestle their vehicles through rich black gumbo. Nothing much in the way of vehicles — horse- or motor-powered — moved on those roads. Iowa's roads were a national joke — in 1920 the entire state had 25 miles of paved highway.

Cowles's persistence helped boost Iowa out of the mud in the Twenties. By 1930, the state had 3,272 miles of paved highway — but it was a difficult as well as a long battle.

As early as 1910, Cowles and Ingham were pushing for better roads. A 1912 editorial unsuccessfully recommended a state bond issue of $25 million to build highways. In 1915, another editorial declared: "All Iowa today is in the throes of a mud blockade. Farmers today are unable to market their hogs. ... Iowa has been practically untravelable and that too after we have built the best dirt grades that can be built. Why are we so blind to the facts of the situation and why is Iowa, which has more use for good roads and can better afford good roads than any of these other states, making a virtue of doing nothing?"

The powerful "mud road" forces consisted mainly of farmers and rural property owners who feared that the new highways would greatly increase their property taxes. Ultimately, their fears were unjustified — motor vehicle license fees, taxes on gasoline and federal funds paid for the roads. Although it was never used to pay road-bond principal and interest, the property tax became a guarantee for both.

Opponents accused Cowles of campaigning for hard roads only to speed delivery of his newspapers around the state. Obviously better roads for better distribution were a dollars-and-cents goal — but the long Cowles campaign for paved roads had a strong develop-Iowa thrust as well.

Along with Cowles, who had the state's largest and most influential newspapers at his command, others who advanced the cause of hard roads included Chief Engineer Fred White of the Iowa Highway Commission, who set a great example nationally in promoting and building new highways; Glenn Haynes, who ran the Iowa Good Roads Association, and Gov. John Hammill, who pushed hard in the late 1920s for highway-building programs.

C. C. Clifton, who covered Iowa Senate activities for *The Register*, wrote hundreds of what amounted to pro-highway stories for *The Register*. Fledgling reporter Gardner (Mike) Cowles, jr., 22 and fresh out of Harvard, covered the highway fight in the Iowa House in 1925. Meanwhile, *Register* Editor Harvey Ingham wrote many pro-highway editorials, as did D. W. Norris of the *Marshalltown Times-Republican,* another ardent good-roads advocate.

In 1919, the Iowa Legislature designated 6,500 miles of roads as the state's primary highway system and took the first steps toward shifting control of these main roads from the county authorities to the state highway commission.

Generaling his roads campaign, Cowles ordered a large map of Iowa posted on a wall outside his office. "Every time a mile or two of new paving was laid, we had to record that fact in colored crayon on the map," a veteran employee said. "We were supposed to keep that map right up to date."

One of the by-products of the *Register* campaign, since the commission did not publish highway maps then, was that *The Sunday Register* often devoted a full page to such a statewide map for the convenience of motorists.

Roads were known by name rather than number, the "River-to-River Road" carried drivers from Davenport to Des Moines to Omaha, the "Hawkeye Highway" ran from Dubuque to Sioux City and motorists used the "Lincoln Highway" to drive from Clinton to Missouri Valley via Cedar Rapids and Marshalltown.

Despite distribution problems, circulation grew rapidly during World War I. The Cowles papers enjoyed the same circulation prosperity that other papers around the country reported as the hunger for war news boomed circulation figures. Des Moines' growth also helped increase circulation; the city gained 40,000 population in 10 years, moving from 86,000 in 1910 to 126,000 in 1920.

Once the war had ended, the demand for newspapers slipped; the combined circulation of the daily *Register* and *Tribune* dropped from a high of 116,000 in 1918 to 106,000 in 1919, then revived to 110,000 in 1920. *The Sunday Register* continued its upward trend, rising from 27,000 in 1910 to nearly 73,000 in 1919.

Toward the end of the war, the papers' circulation planners also had to deal with the effects of inflation.

In early 1917, subscribers paid only 15 cents a week for *The Register, The Tribune* and *The Sunday Register.* The inflation of an America at war soon boosted the price of a single copy of *The Sunday Register* from a nickel to eight cents. (At the same time, the Des Moines Street Railway company ran an ad heatedly denying any intention of raising the streetcar fare in the city from a nickel to six cents.)

By May, 1918, the daily *Register* price was $5 a year or 50 cents a month and *The Sunday Register* was $3 a year or 30 cents a month.

Competition was another major problem. As the "Roaring Twenties" came in, four daily newspapers were competing for readers in Des Moines and central Iowa. Everybody in the business realized that was too many papers in a city of 126,000 population. Pressure grew on editors and reporters to produce lively yet reliable newspapers that would outshine and outlast the competition.

Murders, bombings and other crime, sex and sob stories received good headline play while at the same time newspaper campaigns for better highways and against intolerance and governmental corruption stimulated readership. A revved-up *Tribune* made exciting reading via colorful stories and action photographs, plus lively serial fiction and local columnists like Priscilla Wayne, who was an early version of advice columnist Ann Landers.

Priscilla Wayne — Mrs. Wayne Sprague — was a women's page columnist and feature writer for *The Tribune* and *The Sunday Register* and occasionally for the daily *Register*. She handled letters to *The Tribune* from readers with love or domestic problems, but in her Des Moines career of more than 40 years she also wrote about juvenile delinquency and adoption, about feeding the poor during the Depression and about a woman's interpretation of national political conventions. She held forth on such diverse topics as antiques, dogs, her travels, her home, current events, and fishing, which she loved. In addition, she wrote syndicated serial fiction about youth, love and marriage that ran in newspapers around the country.

A large woman of large energy and imagination, Priscilla Wayne, who died in 1956 at the age of 62, was an important factor in building the readership of the newspapers from the 1920s through the 1940s.

Competition for readership was so stiff that worry over survival permeated newspaper plants.

"The battle for circulation was not confined to the circulation departments," reporter Bill Millhaem said. "Everybody from the news department to the mailing room knew that, directly or indirectly, his job was to sell more papers than the competition.

"The real battle in those days was in street sales. That's where the news department could help most. We manufactured headlines that would sell papers on the street. If we didn't have a good story, we were expected to make one, magnify or expand one. The final edition, which hit the downtown streets late in the afternoon, when workers were taking streetcars for home, had to have headlines that the newsboys could merchandise. We built up feature stories as well as crimes of violence and tales of misfortune. If you could tie into a big headline, the paper would sell."

Sometimes local news and feature coverage became too imaginative — some stories were written in the heat of competition that would not be countenanced in the profession today. Associate Managing Editor William G. (Billy) Hale, one of the most colorful characters on Cowles papers' editing staffs, was responsible for one story in the early 1920s that pointed a moral about overwritten, souped-up stories.

Reporter Rae MacRae wrote a story about an Iowa woman supposedly fatally ill in a hospital, expressing a "deathbed desire" to see her only son, a marine on duty on the Pacific island of Guam, before she died. Hale got an Iowa congressman to urge the Navy to give the marine a leave and the young man headed home on a ship. *The Tribune* played the story for all it was worth — and more — the big question being whether the mother would survive until the son reached Des Moines. Although reporter MacRae meanwhile had reconsidered and said she thought the mother might last quite a while, Billy Hale chose to believe her initial story.

When the marine's ship docked in San Francisco, he got on the first available transcontinental train and headed toward home, at which point then-reporter Rodney Selby, who by virtue of having taken some flying lessons was the paper's aviation editor, suggested that the paper fly the marine into Des Moines from Omaha on a kind of "mercy flight."

"We were all set," as Selby recalled it. "The train from the west was to arrive in Omaha early in the afternoon. We flew to Omaha early in the morning. We were prepared to whisk the boy to his mother's bedside, a spectacular climax to a wonderfully warm story."

It was a story that sold papers in those days; editors at *The News* and *The Capital* writhed with envy.

The day was clear, the temperature 8 below zero. Selby and Rusty Graham, pilot of the three-place plane, had to heat the craft's crankcase oil and the radiator water on an old potbellied stove before taking off from Des Moines. The bone-chilling cold in the open cockpit on the way to Omaha was only the first unpleasantness about the trip. Selby and Pilot Graham landed at the old Ak-sar-ben field, then being used by the U.S. Army. The officer in charge refused to sell the two the gasoline necessary for their return flight; against regulations, he said. Gasoline was delivered from downtown Omaha, and then the marine arrived, wearing a uniform suitable for warm Guam but not below-zero Omaha.

"The boy and I got into the front cockpit," Selby said. "Rusty was in the pilot's seat behind. We started downfield and gained speed. Everything sounded great. We took off near the end of the field and were perhaps 50 feet above the ground when the engine started to cough and miss. I looked back at Rusty. There was a grove of trees dead ahead. I pointed to the ground and nodded my head. Rusty turned the plane on one wing and nosed it down. We crashed on one wing, rolled over on the nose and then on the other wing."

On the way down, Selby had decided he was not going to be in the plane "when it caught fire."

"It didn't catch fire but I wasn't in it either when it came to rest," Selby said. "I'll bet I broke all records for the sitting broad jump. When I picked myself up some 20 feet from the plane. I saw Rusty and the boy hanging upside down by their straps in the fuselage. Miraculously, nobody was hurt. The plane was a wreck."

Selby and the marine took a night train home from Omaha.

"We returned in ignominy," Selby said. "The other papers had a field day telling the world how we had nearly killed the boy after the government had moved heaven and earth to get him home to his dying mother."

The Tribune played down the final story, but that wasn't the worst of it. "We buried the story but we didn't bury the mother," Selby said many years later. "She staged a miraculous recovery. So far as I know, she may *still* be alive."

The Cowles-Ingham papers throve on the stiff competition. One of the Sunday paper's talking points was its magazine section — a razzmatazz conglomeration of rapid-fire pieces, sex-oriented articles and photographs, Iowa features, stories about ghastly criminals. It was printed on ordinary newsprint but the big illustrations often were flashily presented in color. Part of the time, the sections editor was Laura Lou Brookman, an excellent fiction writer herself. In addition to putting out the magazine, she also produced the brown-ink, slick-paper, full-page Sunday rotogravure section, predecessor of today's *Des Moines Sunday Register* Picture Magazine.

The roto section was one of Gardner Cowles's major coups in competition with *The Capital,* which had announced with considerable fanfare in early 1919 that it would start publishing a Sunday paper with Iowa's first Sunday roto section. *The Capital's* four-page picture roto section did appear, on Apr. 6, 1919, but it was not Iowa's first. Gardner Cowles's *Sunday Register* had appeared Mar. 30, the Sunday before, with a brand-new "photogravure" section of *eight* pages.

After reading of *The Capital's* plans, Cowles had hurried to Buffalo, N. Y., where he signed a contract for the new picture section. Three of *The Capital's* four pages contained photographs, local shots of construction on the Hotel Fort Des Moines and Hotel Savery nearing completion in Des Moines and a picture of wrestling champion Earl Caddock of Anita, in Army uniform in France. The larger *Register* section lacked Iowa pictures — there hadn't been time enough — but it did feature pleasant photographs of famed American mothers and their children, beauties of the silent movies and scenes of postwar Europe. Later in the Twenties, the section usually ran to 10 pages, concentrating on pictures and advertising and using little story material. Photographs — local, state, national and international — were its stock in trade.

But however much frills and "human-interest" stories were stressed, the Cowles papers also reported the important and significant news of the era: economic and political news, farm stories, repeal in 1921 of the law forbidding the sale of cigarettes in Iowa as well as an international conference in 1921 and 1922 in Washington, D. C., held to agree on a reduction in naval strength of the great powers.

The latter subject gave Harvey Ingham opportunity to demonstrate his by-now-crystalized viewpoint — "liberal" and internationalist. *The Register* was happy with the reduction agreements, but Ingham warned in an editorial: "Nobody can shut his eyes to the fact that treaties do not enforce themselves . . . . Does it not come home to everyone . . . that the further we go for world organization the more persistent the other nations are for the League of Nations?"

As the Twenties unrolled, the Cowles papers began piling up irreversible gains over the other papers in Des Moines. By 1924, *The News,* long an intense rival of the afternoon *Tribune,* had declined to 27,000 circulation daily while *The Tribune* was selling 65,000 daily.

Roy Howard, head of the Scripps-Howard chain, which owned *The News,* came to Des Moines and invited Gardner Cowles to a conference in the Hotel Fort Des Moines. John Cowles, second of the three Cowles sons and 26 at the time, accompanied his father.

"Roy first gave us a lot of bull about how he was going to build *The News* into the greatest paper in town," John Cowles said. "I suppose he was trying to scare my father." Howard suggested that Gardner Cowles might like to buy *The News.* Cowles said he might. Howard said the paper was worth several million dollars. Cowles replied: "Not to me it isn't." Howard asked what Cowles would give for it, and Cowles's reply was "$150,000," an offer clearly based on Gardner Cowles's knowing both his market and his target's business potentialities.

"Howard screamed about how ridiculous such a price would be," John Cowles said. His father added calmly that Howard could keep the equipment for use by other papers in his chain, since *The News* would be discontinued in the event Cowles bought it. When Howard fretted about possible suits by merchants over canceled advertising contracts, Cowles said he would assume responsibility for any such contracts if Howard would cut the price to $149,000. Howard complained, but accepted the offer.

Announcing the purchase of *The News* and its consolidation with *The Tribune* on Nov. 8, 1924, a *Tribune* statement said:

"The fact that the editorial policies of both papers have been liberal and progressive makes the consolidation particularly fitting. The consolidated paper will strive always for fairness in its news and editorial columns and show sympathy for the average man."

The merger left *The Capital* as the only non-Cowles daily in Des Moines. Meanwhile, the combined circulation of the daily *Register* and *Tribune* rose from 147,329 in 1924 to 164,958 in 1925.

The Twenties were filled with important news stories. One of them, the Sacco-Vanzetti case, for years engaged the interest and emotions of citizens and readers who argued the guilt or innocence of two Italian immigrants, shoe factory worker and radical agitator Nicola Sacco and fish peddler and anarchist Bartolomeo Vanzetti, arrested in 1920 as prime suspects in the killing of two men in a payroll robbery in South Braintree, Mass.

Convicted of murder and sentenced to death, they died in the electric chair in 1927 after more than six years of legal battles and protests of the verdict from throughout the world, from conservatives as well as left-wing and liberal forces.

The Register was of two minds about the case. Cartoonist Jay Darling, who believed the two were guilty, drew a cartoon headed: "The victims of Sacco and Vanzetti had no trial or reprieve." The drawing, published after the executions, pictured two men fleeing a robbery scene, one of them shooting at two victims.

The ramifications of the case clearly troubled Ingham. On Aug. 24, 1927, a *Register* editorial assessed the case, finding some solace in the fact that some conservatives had been drawn to the defense of the accused men. Entitled "Sacco-Vanzetti," the editorial read, in part:

"Sacco and Vanzetti, two men, are now out of the world forever. Sacco and Vanzetti, as two symbols, are reborn into it. America as a whole is going to be regrettably misunderstood. Not radicals alone, but millions unradical, will see us as persecutors. We can emphasize, to combat that judgment, nothing more valuable than the fact that within our own borders the case became an issue of tremendous interest, enlisting in defense of the accused thousands of unquestioned conservatism, and hundreds of very great eminence in true conservative circles.

"The delay of seven years has been emphasized as disgraceful, and so it was, so far as criminal court procedure is concerned. But in another way it was a testimonial to the fact that even in a state with archaic laws governing some parts of its criminal court procedure, it was not possible to execute two anarchists, the fairness of whose conviction for murder was doubted, until after a long series of battles that finally did compel some mighty sober second thought.

"The battle for a complete retrial was lost, indeed, and there are many who deplore it — many who have no sympathy whatever with radicalism of any kind. But the fact that it could be made in America, that it was made, and that it did enlist not an inconsiderable share of our conservatives along with our liberals is the ameliorating fact."

In the political arena, Ingham and Cowles strongly opposed Warren Gamaliel Harding in the race for the 1920 Republican presidential nomination. At the nominating convention in Chicago, Cowles and Ingham backed Illinois Gov. Frank O. Lowden, a native of Iowa's Hardin County, a classmate of Ingham at the University of Iowa and a fighter for the cause of agriculture. After nine ballots, the convention found itself deadlocked between Governor Lowden and Gen. Leonard Wood. In the original "smoke-filled" back room, party leaders selected Ohio newspaperman and businessman Harding as a compromise candidate and put out word at the convention that Harding would be nominated on the tenth ballot. When the Iowa delegation, which had been even more pro-Lowden than his own Illinois delegation, announced it had switched its votes to Harding, the Lowden cause had lost and Harding went on to win the nomination.

Three weeks later, in San Francisco, bitter strife broke out in the Iowa delegation to the Democratic National Convention. Edwin T. Meredith, Des Moines publisher of *Successful Farming* magazine and President Wilson's secretary of agriculture in 1920, was Iowa's favorite-son candidate for that year's Democratic presidential nomination. Meredith's strategy was to back William Gibbs McAdoo of California, son-in-law of President Woodrow Wilson, hoping that McAdoo would choose Meredith as the vice-presidential nominee. Many important Iowa Democrats felt that their party could carry Iowa with a McAdoo-Meredith ticket. But National Committeeman Wilbur Marsh of Waterloo controlled the Iowa delegation, whose 26 votes eventually helped nominate James M. Cox, newspaper publisher and reformist governor of Ohio.

Usually the Cowles papers backed Republican presidental candidates, but in 1920 the papers supported neither major-party candidate. For one thing, Cowles and Ingham disliked the evasiveness of the Republican League of Nations platform plank, which recommended "agreement among nations to preserve the peace ... without compromising national independence." They also objected to the way Harding sometimes talked in circles. After he spoke in Des Moines, *The Register* commented editorially that he did not commit himself to "much of anything." It added: "Perhaps the moral most applicable is the old one: If a man does not have much to say, the better way is not to say it."

But Harding's campaign slogan, urging "a return to normalcy" of the prewar days, appealed to an America and an Iowa that had become isolationist despite vigorous editorial stands of internationalist writers like Ingham. The people at that stage wanted no part of the League of Nations.

Cox strongly supported President Wilson's foreign policy, especially his support of the League. That backing was instrumental in Cox's resounding election loss to Harding, who won 16 million votes nationally to Cox's 9 million, and 635,000 to Cox's 228,000 in Iowa.

In 1924, the marathon Democratic National Convention in New York City took 16 days and a record 103 ballots to nominate John W. Davis to oppose incumbent Calvin Coolidge, who had succeeded to the presidency when Warren Harding died in 1923. Though Republican-oriented, the Cowles papers again did not endorse the GOP candidate. Nor did they back Democrat Davis or the third-party Progressive candidate, Wisconsin's U.S. Senator Robert LaFollette.

Other news centered on the sensational "thrill killing" of young Bobby Franks by two Chicago university students, Nathan Leopold and Richard Loeb; the tragic, futile 20-day struggle to free Floyd Collins, trapped by a rock slide deep in a Kentucky cave; Tennessee's Scopes "monkey trial" over the teaching of the theory of evolution in public schools; the nonstop, 3,600-mile solo flight across the Atlantic Ocean in May, 1927 of "Lucky Lindy," Charles A. Lindbergh, from Mineola, N. Y., to Paris, France in 33½ hours in a Ryan monoplane named "The Spirit of St. Louis."

Commenting upon the Scopes case, in which John Scopes was fined $100 for illegally teaching the theory of evolution in the schools of Dayton, Tenn., *The Tribune* discussed witch-burning and other attacks inspired by fear of the unknown. It said:

"Truth of course will survive for further revelations, but there is a lesson to school boards, legislators and the general public in the Dayton case. That lesson already has been brought home to many. It was stated by the president of Princeton University, himself thoroughly orthodox, in regard to evolution nine years after Darwin enunciated the theory. He declared that religion and science could never be in conflict, that nothing should impede the search for truth because of the principle of the unity of knowledge.

'Tennessee and America are in a way to learn this lesson. Meantime, if they are not burning witches in Tennessee they are fining them."

The Register put the Lindbergh flight in the context of its world-view. Its editorial on Lindbergh's May 20-21, 1927 solo flight over the Atlantic was entitled "Contact." It read:

"When a pilot is ready and ignition is required to start the plane's engine, the call is 'Contact!'

"In making an unbroken flight from America to Europe [Lindbergh] has bound in new proximity two great continents, turning on the ignition for a new phase of social contacts.

"What Lindbergh has done is to make a beginning along a new line in the movement that is making a world community.

"The thought his achievement suggests concerns the futility of barriers between peoples, the inevitability of a continuing, and of necessity an increasingly ordered, contact."

Cowles's and the *Register*'s outward-looking stance was characterized by their attitude toward air travel. The growth of the Air Age intoxicated readers and newsmen of the Twenties just as the early American space flights in the Sixties drew thousands of spectators to Florida's Cape Canaveral. In 1930, *The Register* sent reporter Harlan Miller on a 20,000-mile plane trip around North and South America. The paper said Miller's month-long trip was undertaken "in the belief that within the lifetime of people now living, there will be extensive air traffic between the American Midwest and South America." Read today, Miller's copy constitutes a report on the beginning of airline travel. He flew on 25 airlines, from Winnipeg, in Canada's Manitoba Province, to Buenos Aires, Argentina, visited 24 countries and flew a total of 5,000 miles over water, then considered foolhardy. He wrote about everything from an Argentinian shooting tragedy to the South American reaction to Uncle Sam as a Western Hemisphere bully to the belief that rich Latin American leaders did not want American technology coming into their countries because they wanted to continue paying low wages to their workers.

He wrote light and airy copy, too, about Southern Hemisphere customs, and offered what now sounds like gee-whiz reactions to the wonders of aviation. The public loved the flight stories — when Miller landed in Des Moines at the end of the trip, 3,500 citizens, including Mayor Parker Crouch, met him at the airport.

The stereotype of the "Roaring Twenties" fails to take into account the unhealthy economic conditions that prevailed and the feeling long before the gigantic stock market crash of 1929 that the nation and the state were in severe economic difficulties.

Bad business conditions prevailed in the banking and insurance fields and in merchandising well before Black Tuesday, Oct. 29, 1929.

Des Moines' two largest department stores, Younkers and Harris-Emery, in 1926 decided to merge. That consolidation was a heavy blow to the Des Moines newspapers; the stores were the biggest advertisers in the city. "They began to cut back their advertising space greatly," John Cowles said. Each no longer wanted a page in all of the Des Moines papers for every major sales campaign.

In the face of the reduced advertising, Lafayette Young, jr., publisher of *The Capital*, suggested to John Cowles that the rival papers consolidate. "We were all for a merger, but we didn't want any joint stock deal because my father and Lafe Young, jr., didn't hit it off at all," John Cowles said. "Lafe wanted to sell for cash anyway, so there really was no need to pursue the merger idea." John Cowles handled the transaction for his father, who was traveling with Mrs. Cowles by ocean liner to the Far East.

Young Cowles was in a position to talk cash because of his father's longtime conservative financial philosophy; the elder Cowles had accumulated $300,000 in cash plus some government bonds. The Register and Tribune Company had no difficulty in borrowing the additional amount needed, even though financial times were difficult. John notified his father by radio telegraph of the negotiations and the price, which John Cowles put at $750,000.

"Father was very restless at being away at such a time," John Cowles said. "He was very happy with the deal, though. He would have paid more than that."

The sale, announced Feb. 12, 1927, left *The Register* and *The Tribune* without daily newspaper competition in Des Moines, and the Cowles afternoon paper became, temporarily, *The Tribune-Capital.* Questioning whether getting a monopoly on daily newspapers in Des Moines was a good idea, Gardner Cowles wrote to son John from the Far East expressing worry that *The Register* and *The Tribune* might lose the friendship of many Des Moines residents and that it might be "four or five years before we will know if it was the right thing to do."

Fred Pownall, who had been editor of *The Capital,* said many Des Moines residents were unhappy over the loss of *The Capital.* "There was the natural and usual public reaction," he said, "that comes with the passing of a long-established and well-known citizen — or newspaper."

To meet criticism, the Cowleses set up a Bureau of Accuracy and Fair Play and adroitly chose *The Capital*'s Pownall to run it. Pownall spent full time handling public complaints about stories in the newspapers, about the advertising and about subscription mixups. He said the bureau "had smooth sailing, thanks to the attitude of individuals in all departments, and especially to the co-operation of the management."

(After several months with the bureau, Pownall moved to Iowa City, where he accepted a job as "university editor" and taught journalism at the University of Iowa. Later he was university director of publications and director of student publications. In the latter post, he was publisher of *The Daily Iowan,* the student newspaper.)

With the *Tribune-Capital* merger came immediate rumblings that competing newspapers would be established in Des Moines. A *Des Moines Herald* was organized partway but never printed an issue; other moves to establish rival papers failed, too.

A competitor did appear in January, 1938, *The Des Moines Daily Dispatch,* which had begun in 1933 as a weekly. Operating problems forced it to transform itself back into a weekly, *The Iowa Dispatch-Democrat,* in July of the same year. No competing newspapers have emerged since then, but television and radio have competed forcefully for the advertising dollar. On the newspaper front, the Cowles papers always have faced intense circulation competition from the 40 other daily newspapers in the state.

One of the major stories of the Twenties and Thirties — which *The Register* covered extensively and well because the situation concerned Iowans so directly — was the downfall of banking institutions in essentially rural states like Iowa. Human grief and despair are contained in bank figures of the 15-year era from 1920 to the middle Thirties: At the peak of the farm boom in 1919-1920, Iowa was grossly oversupplied with banks, 1,900 of them, one for each 1,260 of the state's 2.4 million inhabitants. Some small towns had three or four banks.

By 1935, more than 1,200 of those banks had failed or merged; fewer than 650 survived. When a bank failed, depositors lost sizable percentages of their money because there was no minimum guarantee of deposits; the Federal Deposit Insurance Corp. did not exist until the Banking Act of 1933 went into effect.

Nineteen Iowa banks reportedly closed on one day during the 1920s, and between 1920 and 1935 the average Iowa county lost more than a dozen banks. Iowa Gov. Nate Kendall (1921-1925) laid the problem to excessive loans both to individual borrowers and to bank officials, and, he said, banks had taken too many mortgages on real estate already heavily encumbered.

Ruinously low farm prices also battered the economy. Hogs sold for only $6 a hundredweight in December, 1921, and again in June, 1923. Farmers got an average of only 31 cents a bushel for corn and $5.70 per hundredweight for cattle late in 1921.

The proliferation of banks and the blight that attacked them were almost altogether a rural phenomenon. Before World War I, Iowa had more banks than either New York or Illinois. A survey of bank failures for 1921-1926 showed Iowa, with 263 bank failures, second only to North Dakota, with 317. South Dakota had 250 and Minnesota 215. By comparison, New York State and Illinois fared better, New York having had only eight bank failures in the 1921-26 period and Illinois 48.

State and national legislators attempted to meet the problems. The 1923 Iowa Legislature tightened state banking laws and the federal government established an agricultural credit act in 1925, including creation of credit facilities for farmers. That moved Republican Gov. John Hammill (1925-31) to say: "What the farmers want to hear is not where they can borrow more money but how they can pay what they owe. . . . You do not get a man out of debt by getting him in more."

Strong sentiment built up through the Midwest for some sort of bank laws to protect depositors against loss. As early as 1909, Nebraska enacted a law under which depositor-guarantees were financed by a small tax collected on the deposits of all banks. Bankers fought the idea, maintaining that such an insurance plan led to the organization of many unsound banks, whose failures would be paid for by good banks.

With his usual clarity of vision and his customary emphasis on sound foundations to any project, Harvey Ingham was an early supporter of the idea of guaranteeing deposits, but under rigid safeguards. Such guarantees did not undermine the banking system, he said in 1909, but established greater security for their depositors and the banks themselves. If the current state requirements were not stiff enough "to insure stable and reliable banking," he said, "then examinations should be much more rigid and regulations more stringent."

The Nebraska experience was sad; its depositor-guarantee fund was $20 million in the red by 1930. Earlier, in 1927, Ingham was dubious about the whole idea. He wrote that year:

"Unsound banking, speculative banking, banking that disregards the rule about loaning to bank officers and favored customers, or too many banks . . . will break the state under a bank guaranty law just as readily as without such a law.

"With sound banking, a bank guaranty law becomes secondary. Without sound banking, guaranteeing deposits will not meet the situation in a year bad enough to make reliance on the guarantee important."

Reporter Cy Clifton's coverage kept Iowans abreast of the banking situation. In a 1927 story, he wrote that only four of the closed banks returned 100 per cent of depositors' funds upon liquidation of the bank; 16 others returned 75 per cent and the majority were expected to pay only 50 per cent of original total deposits. In 1929, Clifton reported that depositors had lost $30 million in 248 state banks that had gone into receivership in the preceding six years. Those banks had reported combined total deposits of $64 million.

In the midst of the long banking crisis, the Iowa Loan and Trust Co., a Des Moines bank, found itself in difficulty because it had made some poor real estate loans. When word got around, depositors began making heavy withdrawals, and when the bank closed normally for the weekend one Saturday in December, 1926, the vault contained less than $100,000. Des Moines business and financial leaders worked desperately over the weekend to save the bank. Publisher Gardner Cowles agreed to put up a major sum — estimated by John Cowles at upward of $200,000 — and Norman Wilchinski, president of Younkers department store, pledged an equal amount.

The finance effort went on until 3 a.m. Monday, but when eastern insurance interests for which Iowa Loan and Trust had guaranteed some $5 million in mortgages would not release the bank from its obligation, the bank could not be saved. It did not open that Monday morning.

The failure touched off "runs" on at least two other banks. Iowa National, the city's biggest bank, withstood heavy withdrawals but at Des Moines National, which in fact was weaker than the failing Iowa Loan and Trust, a clever tactic devised by Board Chairman Louis Kurtz, a hardware merchant and a Catholic, helped save the bank.

As depositors thronged into Kurtz's bank that Monday morning bent on making withdrawals, Kurtz put his plan in motion. John Cowles, on the scene because he had agreed to accept appointment to Des Moines National's board to bolster the bank's prestige, tells the story:

"Kurtz got two priests to keep coming into the bank, not to make withdrawals but to make deposits of currency. The priests kept going around making additional deposits. Louie asked them to be very slow about it and to make themselves as prominent as possible inside the bank. The idea was to demonstrate that the Catholic Church had confidence in the stability of the bank. Each priest spread bills and coins around when he reached the teller window. Every time, the priest told the teller to be very slow in counting the cash.

"All of this slowed up the withdrawals and kept a lot of people standing in line for long periods of time. This caused many to say to themselves: 'I've been here an hour and a half. I'll take a chance and go away.' "

Des Moines National survived and later consolidated with Iowa National to form the present Iowa-Des Moines National Bank.

While the Cowles papers made extensive efforts to provide comprehensive coverage on subjects like the banking crisis, there was still soul-searching about Des Moines' having become a "one-paper town" dominated by the Cowles family. The situation prompted the *Tribune-Capital* to issue a policy statement at the time of the merger in 1927 that promised coverage with "a sense of justice and fair play to the public." It added: "The theory of *The Tribune-Capital* will be that the people of Iowa are entitled to know what happens and that they are thoroughly competent to form their own opinions on the basis of full information." The merger was "in line with the clear trend toward fewer, larger and better newspapers," the statement added.

Combined circulation of the Cowles papers at merger time in February, 1927, was 222,292 daily and 161,879 Sunday. Final issues of *The Capital* carried no circulation figures. A comparison of figures before and after the merger indicates the gain for *The Tribune,* as well as the progress of her sister papers.

	1926 Circulation	1927 Circulation
Sunday Register	106,640	118,184
Daily Register...............	69,978	79,368
Daily Tribune..............	48,383	73,499

With the field clear, Gardner Cowles did not lean back and relax. In his unpublished history of *The Register,* W.C. Dewel wrote:

"After a long struggle, Gardner Cowles was master of the field — but the many who expected him to let down were mistaken. He did not rest because he could not. He knew that rest was fatal. He started out to make a state paper for Iowa's 2.5 million people that would far surpass anything previously achieved."

How well he, his sons, Harvey Ingham, circulation man William Cordingley and the rest of the staff succeeded in building such newspapers is demonstrated by circulation figures for the 1928-1941 period, which included the worst depression in United States history. Combined circulation of the two dailies increased from 226,318 in 1928 to 313,103 in 1941, an over-all gain of nearly 87,000.

The Sunday paper's advance was more spectacular still — from 168,671 to 376,372, a rise of more than 207,000 circulation in 14 years.

Gardner Cowles's effective personnel choices were not confined to editorial or circulation employees. He also knew a good man with figures when he saw one.

One of his happy selections began unhappily, costing the Register and Tribune Company upward of $50,000 *before* Cowles hired his man. Arthur Gormley became the firm's auditor in 1928, but he had come to Iowa in 1922 as a U.S. Internal Revenue Service agent, drawing the assignment of auditing the newspapers on an income tax question. An in-house audit had determined that the company owed $15,000 or $16,000 in back taxes; meanwhile a New York auditor told company officials that the firm had a slight refund coming.

But IRS agent Gormley figured "everything from a very strict Internal Revenue position, as was my duty," and he "came up with a figure of $175,000 or $180,000 owed by the company, which was a hell of a lot of money." Gormley, of course, knew "that many things should be compromised, legitimately." He said: "Gardner Cowles had been operating the newspapers on an extremely conservative basis. When he bought and paid for some second-hand machinery, he charged it to current expense. There was no such thing as invested capital."

The situation was, Gormley said, "extremely complicated, involving almost every angle of the income tax law." The case went to the district office at Omaha and then to Washington, and the final assessment, Gormley said, "was upward of $50,000, which was paid."

Having been through the auditing process with the IRS man, the Cowleses realized Gormley had financial know-how the paper needed. In 1928, Gormley took the auditor post, soon becoming a key man in the Cowles papers' operation. In 1936, he was named business manager. When he retired in 1960, he was vice-president of the company as well.

Meanwhile, while the business department was prospering, gambits to increase circulation continued in the Twenties. The biggest Iowa gimmick of the lot was one of young Mike Cowles's ideas, which eventually involved 15,000 Iowa children contributing nickels and dimes to buy a small elephant all their own, eventually named "Baby Mine." Youngsters sent in nearly $1,000 in coins to *The Register* and *Tribune*. The papers paid most of the rest of the animal's $3,600 price.

The Cowles papers and the Iowa State Fair Board jointly sponsored the project, aimed at the twin goals of increasing the papers' circulation totals and stimulating attendance at the fair. It did both, but in later years, the gimmick wearied editors, the Fair Board, and if truth were known, readers as well. For one thing, the "cute little" Indian pachyderm insisted on growing. Upon arrival in Des Moines, "Baby Mine" measured four feet high and weighed 1,160 pounds. Her weight doubled, then tripled. "The beast was eating her head off," said a State Fair official. "The darn critter ate a bale of hay a day. She was eating us out of house and home." "Baby Mine" performed for little more than a week at the fair each year, but of course had to be maintained all year long. By 1942, the Fair Board was glad to sell her for $750 and contribute the money to Iowa Lutheran Hospital's polio clinic.

Another promotion stunt, less successful, involved the use in the mid-1930s of pigeons to fly news pictures back to Des Moines from the Fort Madison state penitentiary, where a prisoner was scheduled to be hanged. Reporter Gordon Gammack and photographer Maurice Horner took two homing pigeons the 180 miles from Des Moines to Fort Madison. Horner made the customary shots — of the prisoners emerging from Death Row and, later, of their shroud-covered bodies. After the execution, Horner placed his negatives into capsules, attached them to the birds' legs, and sent the pigeons off toward Des Moines. They never arrived.

On the editorial side, the death penalty and the Cowles papers' photo coverage of proceedings surrounding executions prompted a June 6, 1935 editorial that said: "No doubt some people found those pictures horrible. They were. The thing they so meticulously represented was horrible, that is why. If society doesn't like things like this, society has both the power and the responsibility to prevent them. Merely turning the gaze away does not alter the realities."

7 THE COWLES BROTHERS

When the Eagle Grove *Eagle*'s Ward Barnes analyzed the success of *The Register* in terms of autonomous units and allegiance to the Cowles family, he put his finger on the key to Gardner Cowles's and Harvey Ingham's continuing success.

The Cowles sons, John and Mike — coming out of Harvard in 1920 and 1925, respectively — in a dozen ways helped spark the accelerated Twenties growth of the Cowles papers. Average daily circulation of *The Register* and *The Tribune* more than doubled in the decade, from 111,000 in 1920 to 243,000 in 1930, while *The Sunday Register*'s circulation average rose from 86,000 to 206,000.

Staffs were expanded, picture usage brightened the pages, *Register* sports and farm news coverage improved, the papers used their airplanes to good advantage in covering the news, and John Cowles launched the Register and Tribune Syndicate, which has been highly successful in selling features and services to other papers ever since.

Growth was the order of the decade, and the Cowles sons were responsible for much of it. "Gardner Cowles built a solid newspaper foundation," said business manager Arthur Gormley, "but he was fortunate to have his sons coming up. . . . The old gentleman and Harvey were good, but the boys gave the paper a push that kept them going upward."

Of Gardner and Florence Cowles's six children, three sons and three daughters, the two younger sons, John and Mike, were to become deeply involved in the publishing world. John was born Dec. 24, 1898 and Gardner, jr.(Mike) Jan. 31, 1903 at Algona. The eldest of the three brothers, Russell, born Oct. 7, 1887, also at Algona, opted out of the newspaper business early.

Interested in art and nature, Russell found his father's

stress on games of mental arithmetic and on business too much for him. "My father and I didn't hit it off very well when I was growing up," Russell said. "When I was 10 or 12 years old, I felt closer to my mother, who was more sympathetic with my interest in art. My father rubbed me the wrong way sometimes. As a boy I also . . . was interested in ornithology. My father just wasn't interested, nor did he care one way or the other when I went out for track at Algona High School." What made Russell unhappiest was his father's reaction to his high school report cards. "If I came home with a card showing four *A*s and one *B*, he would say: 'What about that *B*?' He did not mention the four *A*s." Russell also fumed because his father, like *his* father before him, required the boy to work on a farm in summertime.

"My father said every young man should work on a farm at some time or other," Russell Cowles said. "I had to, but he never required my brothers, John and Mike, to do so. The oldest gets the worst of it."

Gardner Cowles was disappointed when Russell refused to stay with *The Register and Leader* after being graduated in 1909 from Dartmouth College and told a job was waiting for him in the classified ad department. "I thought I would be more interested in news and editorial writing," Russell Cowles said. "My father wanted me to join the business department. He was carrying a pretty heavy load [and] . . . wanted someone to take part of that burden off his shoulders."

Russell Cowles spurned the job and went to France to study art. "My father didn't think much of that idea," he said. "He gave me only a limited amount of money for my stay in Paris. When the money was gone, I came home and went to work in Classified . . . . After less than two years, I couldn't take it any more. I went to New York and enrolled in an art school."

In 1915, Russell Cowles, an accomplished muralist, won the prestigious Prix de Rome, which included a three-year fellowship for study in Rome. Thus, Russell Cowles was in Rome when the United States entered the war in 1917. He spent the entire war in Rome working as a painter and using that as a "cover" for his other job, as a U.S. naval intelligence agent in Allied Italy. Even more than half a century later, Russell was still following his policy of not speaking about his intelligence activities.

Back home, the Prix de Rome had reconciled Gardner

Cowles to Russell's career in art. "Up to that time," Russell Cowles said, "Father hoped that art was something foolish I would get out of my system and that I ultimately would go into the business." Eventually, Gardner Cowles knew that Russell was lost to newspapering and came around to being rather proud of his son.

Later in life, Russell Cowles and his father developed a warm relationship. "He had a perfectionist standard which the children all automatically inherited," Russell said, summing up his father. "That was an excellent heritage. I'm a perfectionist, too, and that has helped me greatly in art."

In their expanding publishing efforts, John and Mike Cowles operated with a broad newspapering background developed under their father.

They learned not to be parsimonious about funding news coverage, whether in Iowa villages, in Washington, D. C., or in the world at large. Cowles papers always have spent more money getting the news and pictures than most other newspapers their size. *Fortune* magazine once said of the family's operation in Iowa: "... There is nothing in the Cowles' record to indicate that the family ever lusted after power or profits. They were a dyed-in-the-wool newspaper family with an urge, above all, to produce a paper that would honor their craft. That they became publishers of the No. 1 paper was due to their initiative and talent . . . ."

Mike and John centered their entire attention on the family's home newspapers during the 1920s and early 1930s. In 1935, they bought *The Minneapolis Star* and John later moved to Minneapolis to take over as resident publisher. In 1937, Mike launched *Look* magazine. Moving East and keeping an eye on the Des Moines operation from the distance, he continued to guide *The Register* and *The Tribune* in the Forties, the Fifties and the Sixties. Ultimately, the brothers divided their joint interests, Mike running *Look* and the Des Moines operation and John in charge at Minneapolis.

Always close personally and keeping in frequent touch no matter how far separated geographically, John and Mike at the height of their active careers held two or three half-hour telephone conversations weekly, to discuss their usually coinciding viewpoints and to co-ordinate general policy for their publications. They saw eye to eye on most issues — John was once quoted as saying: "Our views are 98 per cent identical on any major subject."

In keeping with their *Register* heritage, John and Mike were deeply interested in foreign affairs. They sensed, far more than many midwesterners of their era, that failure to solve international problems often was followed by the loss of many American lives and the waste of much American wealth in war. They supported, as possible investments in peace, the allocation of large U.S. appropriations for foreign aid, given to needy nations with no strings attached.

Both brothers did a considerable amount of reporting themselves, on a national and world scale, and in numerous trips talked with the great figures of their time: Winston Churchill, Josef Stalin, Konrad Adenauer, King George VI, Charles De Gaulle, Nikita Khrushchev, Herbert Hoover, Franklin D. Roosevelt, Harry Truman, Dwight Eisenhower, John Kennedy, Lyndon Johnson, Richard Nixon.

The Cowles brothers' reports from overseas through the years indicated a deep interest in the world at large and a further commitment to telling their readers about it. *A propos* the interest and the commitment, John Cowles once observed:

"I admit it — we have something approaching a sense of mission."

8 JOHN COWLES

When he took his sons into the business, Gardner Cowles did not do it by half measures. Early in 1923, he appointed John, 24 years old and less than three years out of Harvard, as vice-president, general manager and associate publisher of the Register and Tribune Company. Instead of being mere nepotism, the appointment proved to be one of the best things that happened to the company.

John demonstrated the qualities of an excellent newspaper executive, pushing hard for information, knowledge and knowhow not only in newspapering but also in world affairs. His stock-in-trade was questions. As a prep school student home on vacation from Phillips Exeter Academy in Exeter, N.H., he would come down to the office, sit on the desk of his father's secretary and fire one question after another: "What does Mr. Southwell do? [William B. Southwell was business manager.] Is he smart? . . . What's that voucher for? . . . How much does newsprint cost? . . . How long does it take the press to print 1,000 newspapers? . . ."

He was graduated with honors from Exeter in 1917, enrolled at Harvard that fall, served a brief stint in an Army officer training school at Camp Lee, Va., in 1918, after having (to his later regret) acceded to his parents' wishes that he not join a Harvard ambulance company that ultimately served in the Italian campaign with distinction. He returned to Harvard and completed his AB degree work, with good grades, in June of 1920 instead of 1921. He went out for the Harvard crew with little success, but that was made up for by his becoming the first undergraduate ever to serve as editor of all three Harvard publications, *The Crimson, The Lampoon* and *The Advocate.*

The maturing John Cowles's keenness in business

matters was exceptional, as demonstrated by his launching of the Register and Tribune Syndicate with a goal not only of making additional money but also of nurturing more and better features for the Cowles papers. Of his journalistic expertise, *The New York Herald-Tribune* once said: "He probably knows more detail about every operation right down the line than the men doing the jobs .... He isn't telling funny stories at staff meetings. He's asking questions." Wherever he was, John Cowles maintained close surveillance over the news, regularly reading everything in the papers and demanding accuracy. At Minneapolis, the morning *Tribune* once carried a story with the headline "633 Enrolled at Augsburg." The first sentence said: "Registrations to date show 633 students — 361 male and 212 female — will attend the 1952-53 term at Augsburg College." Apparently only the head man noticed that the figures added up to 573, not 633. Deskmen received a clipping from Cowles's office with a red-penciled note asking: "What sex are the rest?"

John began his apprenticeship in newspapering early. When he was 17, in the summer of 1916, he and a young friend, Tommy Moore, left Des Moines every Monday to solicit farm subscriptions to *The Register* and *The Tribune*. "We had moderate luck selling the papers, but I'd hate to have to live on the commissions we made," he recalled later. "I think we got a dollar or two for every subscription sold. We discovered that the poorer a farm looked, the more likely we were to make a sale." The roads were so muddy that he and his colleague slept in the Cowles car four nights a week rather than try to return to Des Moines after a day's selling.

After he had reached the top of the newspaper business, John Cowles still was not averse, in special circumstances, to going house to house soliciting subscriptions. On merger day, after the Cowleses had bought *The Des Moines News* in 1924, the company wanted to make sure that *The Tribune* was delivered to all former *News* subscribers. Because the papers' city circulation department did not have enough staff members to conduct a house-to-house canvass, John Cowles said, "some of the rest of us pitched in" and found that *The News* "did not have nearly the circulation they said they had." Ultimately, he said, the circulation efforts netted roughly 15,000 or 20,000 new subscribers for *The Tribune,* although *The News* had claimed 40,000 circulation.

As much as he was involved in the business side of the operation, John Cowles also was deeply interested in foreign affairs, partly because he grew up in the midst of World War I and partly as a result of reading his family's internationalist-minded papers. (Harvey Ingham had begun promoting an association of nations as early as 1914.)

John Cowles became a long-time admirer of Woodrow Wilson and his League of Nations peace efforts after attending a 1919 meeting where the president delivered a League-promoting speech. John Cowles also became the closest of the Cowles family to President Herbert Hoover. After Hoover was defeated in the 1932 election by Franklin D. Roosevelt, the ex-president made a cross-country motor trip to his California home, stopping as a guest in the John Cowles home at 50 Thirty-seventh Street in Des Moines, next to the home of the senior Cowleses.

Gardner Cowles and his sons and Harvey Ingham obviously were disappointed at the Hoover defeat. To some extent at least their disappointment paralleled that of early *Register* Editor Ret Clarkson in 1884, but they were much more philosophical than Clarkson, who was so furious that he refused for days to concede that Democrat Grover Cleveland had won the presidency over Republican James G. Blaine, Clarkson's candidate.

A *Register* editorial on the outcome of the Hoover-Roosevelt election said: "*The Register* favored President Hoover principally because of its belief that he is the abler man. . . . Roosevelt is going to have a chance to demonstrate that he is [an] abler man than he was estimated to be, abler than his hazy speeches and want of any concrete program that he was willing to present to the people indicated him to be. . . ."

When Hoover delivered the Drake University commencement address in Des Moines June 3, 1935, he asked John Cowles for recommendations for his speech topic. Cowles responded with a list of suggestions that reflected his own philosophy at the time, focusing on "the opportunity that American life under our traditional economic and social system [holds] for young people who [have] brains and energy and ambition."

A *Tribune* editorial on June 4, 1935, entitled "Hoover at Drake," praised Hoover's philosophy of minimal government control of citizens' lives. It read, in part:

"His advice to the graduates was simply put.

"It was a denial that all adventure or opportunity has

gone out of life. Research, science, invention — the field for pioneers in those fields is not less broad but broader now than before.

"It was a reminder that the youth of today have much more to start with than their fathers, particularly in a region like Iowa, had.

"And it closed with an emphasis on the importance of preserving — of not sacrificing thoughtlessly — the intangible but vital tenets of individual freedom that up to now on this continent men have had — of not succumbing to the habit-forming drug of 'state-isms' — of not letting democracy itself vanish in the effort to grasp more quickly other things — of not selling for a mess of pottage the great birthright of America and of the other English-speaking countries, Liberty."

Next day, a *Register* editorial urged concentration on retaining "free institutions" while correcting "abuses." Entitled "They Who Speak for Liberty," it praised efforts of Hoover and South African statesman Jan Christian Smuts for peace and freedom. Warning of the "danger" of "new Caesarisms," it said:

"When the laudable pursuit of social justice leads to the embracing of methods which seem to promise more immediate results, more "efficiency" in the chase, he who protests that the methods themselves endanger our ideals is likely to be misunderstood as merely one who is negative toward all correction of abuses.

"The great human rights or privileges for which men fought to the death come to be taken completely for granted by later generations, and the words that stand for them lose their meaning. Few are really stirred by 'Liberty.' It seems only a shibboleth." Hoover and Smuts, it added, stand for "the making of democracy more and more workable, but by means which shall leave democracy 'master in his own house.' "

But all of that was well into the future. In 1920, after finishing his Harvard work, John Cowles traveled through Europe with brother Russell for several months. Their adventures ranged from dodging bullets of Benito Mussolini's Fascist blackshirts in Venice's Piazza San Marco to enlarging a taste for art that ultimately led him and his wife, the late Elizabeth Morley Bates Cowles, to assemble in Minneapolis a fine collection of paintings and sculpture.

After his Grand Tour, John Cowles joined the *Register* staff as a reporter and covered the 1921 session of the Iowa

Legislature. He became fascinated with politics, state and national, and from 1920 onward attended major party national conventions until his retirement.

John Cowles began his extensive newspaper travels in 1923, when he succeeded in waiting out the bureaucracy of Communist Russia and making a tour of that nation in its first post-revolutionary phase. In the midst of a "Red scare" at home, he wrote 14 articles giving candid impressions of what he saw. On the whole, he did not find the Russia of 1923 an evil land and concluded that the Bolsheviks, who had "made many social reforms and hope to make more," would stay in power. His balanced Russian reports did not go down well with some readers, and his refusal to endorse a "holy war" against the Soviet Russians prompted the president of the Iowa Bar Association to denounce him as a "red-bellied Bolshevist." Such attacks did not bother him then, or in later life.

Reflecting in the 1970s on political systems, he said: "I think democracy with all its faults is the best system. But if other countries want something different, let them try. A war against Communism is not a holy crusade in any sense." In earlier decades, John Cowles, long an agnostic, took the Roman Catholic Church and Francis Cardinal Spellman to task for advocating a holy war against Communism and in the 1950s he was assailed by *American Legion Magazine* for suggesting U.S. diplomatic recognition of Communist China.

Over the years, John Cowles often asserted that attainment of an enforceable peace, control of human fertility and cultivating better race relations were the three most important problems confronting Twentieth Century humankind. Cowles credited his wife, Elizabeth, whom he married the summer after his return from Russia, with helping him develop his ideas "on the necessity for improving race relations and for halting the world's population growth." The late Mrs. Cowles, a Smith College graduate and widely read in many fields, did not hesitate to say so when she disagreed with the editorial positions of either the Des Moines or the Minneapolis papers.

The move to Minneapolis was an extension in all respects of the Gardner Cowles-Harvey Ingham method of building good newspapers. It started in 1935, when John and Mike concluded that it was time for both of them to branch out from Des Moines. The Cowleses paid $1 million for *The Minneapolis Star,* third and weakest news organization in the city. "My father realized that *The Register* and *The Tribune* [operation] was too small for Mike and me both," John Cowles said. "My father was still more or less active and he had a good organization in Des Moines."

Gardner Cowles and his two newspapering sons first looked at the Paul Block papers in Duluth, Minn., a year or so before buying *The Star,* but "Block wanted too much money and we didn't buy," John said, adding, "Thank God we didn't, because if we had gone to Duluth, we never would have purchased *The Star.*"

Years later, writing about the Minneapolis move, *The New York Herald-Tribune* put it this way: "The *Minneapolis Star* was slowly sinking in the northwest when the Cowleses . . . bought it in 1935. A skinny afternoon sheet, *The Star* was running a poor third in the Minneapolis field of three. People should have paid more attention. Father Cowles had moved into Des Moines on precisely the same gambit a generation earlier; now his *Register* and *Tribune* were alone in the field and dominating Iowa."

Though the comparison was not quite accurate because *The Register* at the time Gardner Cowles acquired it had a better public image than did *The Star,* the Cowles brothers like their father 32 years before felt they knew what they were doing. The rationale for choosing Minneapolis is contained in John Cowles's personal history in Register and Tribune Company files:

"When the Cowles brothers decided to expand outside Des Moines, their first step was to survey available newspapers in other cities. They wanted an evening paper with strong reader loyalty and heavy emphasis on home-delivered circulation. They wanted to find a paper in a community with a high rating for literacy and education, a high percentage of native-born citizens and a relatively even distribution of purchasing power — few rich and few poor. Their search led them to *The Minneapolis Star.*"

Competitors were not frightened. *The Star,* no bargain, was losing money and destined to lose much more. Ultimately, three years of hard promotion got the paper into the black. Although the elder Gardner Cowles supported his sons, "he didn't want the boys to go into Minneapolis," in the opinion of Stuffy Walters. "He summoned some of us and said: 'This is the boys' venture. You are to have nothing to do with it. Your interests are here in Des Moines. Some of you risked your money by buying stock in *The Register* and *Tribune.* We are not going to risk that money. The boys have some money and they can risk their own." Eventually, however, the Register and Tribune Company did acquire stock in the Minneapolis operation, which at the beginning of 1977 amounted to an 11.7 per cent interest.

Conservative, insular, self-protective Minneapolis was a hard nut to crack for the Cowleses. *The Star* recorded sizable gains over its purchase-date circulation of 79,000. By the end of 1935, circulation had reached 100,000 and in early 1936 *The Star* took the lead in want-ad linage over its entrenched competitors, *The Minneapolis Journal* and *The Minneapolis Tribune*, which had an evening edition as well as a large morning operation.

But even though *The Star* by September, 1936, had become the largest evening-circulation paper in the area — 119,000 daily against 118,000 for *The Journal* and 69,000 for the evening edition of *The Tribune* — *The Star* was a losing operation because it was not selling enough display advertising.

The national magazine *Today* in 1937 summed up the problem: "*The Minneapolis Star* . . . . is read by working-men and small retailers who are still rather astonished to find a paper that gives a play to strike news, etc. Advertisers tend to hold off for the same reason, as Minneapolis was one of the storm centers of the 1934 strike wave, and capital-labor lines are sharply drawn." After *The Star*'s 115,000 circulation figure shrank to 100,000, Gardner Cowles, sr., in September, 1937, issued an order to John Cowles and Stuffy Walters to establish residence in Minneapolis. Since 1935, they had been commuting between their Des Moines and Minneapolis jobs. "Mr. Cowles wanted the Minneapolis operation straightened out," Stuffy Walters said. "He said: 'What we should do is build up *The Star* so it can be sold.'"

John Cowles took over the advertising and business departments and Walters, who resigned as *Register* managing editor in October, 1937, became *The Star*'s editor. "John went out and hit the pavement soliciting advertising, which came very slowly," Walters said. "It all was a slow proposition." Personal acceptance was slow, too. "Our next-door neighbors refused to have anything to do with us," Walters recalled. "They regarded anybody working for *The Star* as Communists."

The Star captured attention. "I tell you," Walters said, "the Cowles boys were scared and they let me try anything. We had a small news staff, I think about 33. We had good pictures.... We let the editors and reporters try almost anything.... The very fact that we had only one press service [United Press] proved an asset, because we loaded the paper with local stories and local pictures."

In Minneapolis, the Cowleses continued their resistance to advertiser pressures. After a widely known businessman was arrested on a charge of violating the hunting laws, *The Tribune* and *The Journal* at his request did not print the story, but *The Star* did, to his amazement and dismay. Said John Cowles: "Printing the news greatly stimulated our circulation. It took many years for the business community to get used to the idea that news would be printed regardless of whose interests might be harmed."

In his history of *The Minneapolis Tribune*, newspaperman Bradley L. Morison wrote that he was early made conscious of the news ideals that Cowles, Walters and others brought to Minneapolis from Des Moines.

In "Sunlight on Your Doorstep," Morison wrote: "It was made plain to me almost from the beginning that the newspapers' opinions were to be sharply confined to its editorial columns.... The news was to be presented at all times, to quote Cowles, 'as honestly and fairly and intelligently as possible.' On such occasions as this rule was breached, I am certain it was done without John Cowles's sanction."

Cowles's red pencil was much in evidence — writing "superb" or "fine" on an article he liked or chiding writers like the one whose frivolously critical editorial on Eleanor Roosevelt got a "this isn't amusing" comment. He occasionally sent a note to an editorial writer or reporter saying "I think you went a notch too far" or "You might have gone a notch farther." Such observations were always mild; it is said that no one ever saw John Cowles "real mad." When he suggested that the newspapers take a certain stand, he often said to the editorial writers: "Now, if you fellows agree with this ... " Said Morison: "Sometimes the 'fellows' disagreed, but I never saw him ruffled by dissent."

He took the customary amount of heat from individuals who objected to news stories or editorials but followed the Cowles pattern of not yielding on a good policy or editorial approach. He also did not mention to the editorial writers any of "the fires built under him."

In his foreword to Morison's "Sunlight on Your Doorstep," Minnesota Democratic U.S. Senator Hubert Humphrey captured another aspect of the Cowles approach, when he wrote:

"I respect the standard John Cowles has laid down for his people about separating news and opinion. But I must say I think he fails occasionally. There are times when he just can't resist using his newspapers to tell his readers things he believes they ought to know, even if these happen to be things they had not asked to know. I am glad of this. I have always believed politicians must be partly educators. So, too, should newspapers."

John Cowles spelled out his news and editorial intentions in a Minneapolis statement that said: "We try to keep our news columns objective and we do not editorialize in the news columns. We express our opinions only on the editorial page" which publishes the writings of "a large number of political commentators of divergent opinions."

Taking the same tack as Senator Humphrey, Cowles termed the newspaper "an educational institution with comparable responsibilities" and demanded that "a good newspaper reporter should be as objective and untiring in his pursuit of truth as a scientist doing research work in a university."

In a speech he gave at the University of Missouri, John Cowles emphasized that an outstanding newspaper is never the creation of one man. "If a newspaper is staffed by men of high professional competence, intelligence and character," he said, "men whose basic philosophy is similar, the newspaper is better if the team is driven with loose reins."

Though he consistently encouraged colorful writing in his papers, he acquired the inaccurate image of being colorless personally because he paid so much attention to the business side. One writer called him "about as colorful as a Minnesota snowscape," and a Cowles executive remarked that although John was "just not the type one calls Jack," he still "is warm and respected . . . an idealist who knows how to make money. An egghead — and about as sharp as a razor's edge."

His career was anything but colorless. In 1939, four years after he and his father and brother acquired *The Star,* the paper bought the rival *Journal* and consolidated the two papers under the name *Star-Journal.* The competing *Tribune* put up a stiff fight, but the *Star-Journal* competition grew keener and *Tribune* expenses rose steadily under pressure of World War II inflation. The *Tribune*'s owners offered to buy the Cowles paper, but Gardner Cowles no longer had doubts about the strength of his sons' Minneapolis operation. He said: "We're not selling. We're buying."

The result was the merger of *The Tribune* into *The Star-Journal.*

While he acted primarily in an administrative role, John Cowles continued to report for his papers and to maintain high-level contacts with Republican leaders. In 1941, Wendell Willkie, the unsuccessful Republican presidential candidate in 1940, asked his good friend, John Cowles, to accompany him on a trip to war-besieged Britain.

Out of that trip, John Cowles wrote a series of eight newspaper articles under the title "Britain Under Fire," which ran in 32 U.S. and five Canadian papers and reflected the horror, anxiety, suspense and courage of the British under saturation bombing by Nazi planes. He strongly disagreed with critics who advised halting all aid to Britain because, they believed, she had already been defeated. The series argued that the United States must aid Britain, and it shocked Midwest isolationists and forces that were trying to keep America out of the war. Willkie and Cowles met with British Prime Minister Winston Churchill, King George VI, and Eamon De Valera, president of the Irish Republic.

Later, in April, 1941, eight months before the Japanese attack on Pearl Harbor, Hawaii, plunged the United States into World War II against Japan and Nazi Germany, John Cowles spoke to the Academy of Political Science in New York. Dwelling on an internationalist theme that sprang from the early days of Harvey Ingham and Gardner Cowles, he looked ahead to the end of the war and said that American participation in the war followed by more isolationism would be disastrous.

"Just helping destroy Hitler is of itself not enough," he said. "After Hitlerism is crushed, America must, in its own enlightened self-interest as the most powerful nation in the world, go ahead and exert its full influence to help shape the course of the world, not along past imperialistic lines of human exploitation but in the pattern of freer self-government, wider trade areas and a more secure existence for all peoples everywhere.

"The possibility that the U.S. might enter this war and might then, when victory is won, crawl back into a shell of ignorant, narrow isolationism is something that must be avoided at all costs."

John Cowles's various world and national trips proved

privately and personally instructive as well as publicly useful in the reports he wrote.

In 1951, he traveled to Europe with Paul Hoffman, who was the first chairman of the Committee for Economic Development (CED), a private organization whose goal was creating peacetime jobs after World War II. Hoffman in 1948 became the first head of the U.S. Economic Co-operation Administration, which ran the Marshall Plan's economic program to rebuild Europe after the war. Between periods of public service Hoffman headed the Studebaker Corp. He also was president of the Ford Foundation and later headed the United Nations Development Program.

The purpose of the Cowles-Hoffman trip was to urge Gen. Dwight D. Eisenhower, then in Paris as commander of North Atlantic Treaty Organization forces, to run for the 1952 Republican presidential nomination.

The Republicans, who had not won a presidential election since 1928, badly needed a victory. Hoffman and Cowles found themselves locked in a prolonged series of conferences with Eisenhower in Paris.

"God, Ike played hard to get," John said. "You could tell he really wanted to be President although he kept denying it. There is no question but that President Truman tried to get him for the Democratic nomination. Ike, however, was a Republican and more conservative than I thought he'd be. He was incredibly naive about American politics."

Day after day, Hoffman and John Cowles tried to persuade Eisenhower to commit himself to seeking the nomination. Other pro-Eisenhower Republicans, like Henry Luce, publisher of *Time* and *Life* magazines, also were talking to the general. On the fifth day that Hoffman and John Cowles talked to him, Eisenhower "did say definitely that he would run," Cowles said.

The Cowles papers strongly supported Eisenhower for the presidency in 1952 and 1956 but did not hesitate to criticize his policies. They took issue with his foreign policy and attacked Secretary of State John Foster Dulles, accusing him of "inflexibly trying to preserve the status quo with treaties and military pacts" instead of recognizing changing world-power patterns.

Part of the Cowleses' anti-Dulles feeling may have stemmed from John Cowles's relationship with Dean Acheson, Harry Truman's secretary of state. In 1953, John

Cowles and Acheson talked every day for a month in Antigua, the British West Indies island where Cowles and his wife had built a winter home. Afterward, Cowles rated Acheson as "one of the greatest secretaries of state of the Twentieth Century."

In 1959, John Cowles again was at the center of political events when President Eisenhower asked him to help prevent Vice-President Richard Nixon from getting the 1960 presidential nominaton. In a 1970 interview, John Cowles disclosed that Eisenhower approached him before a 1959 White House dinner.

"The President knew that we [John and Mike Cowles] had been instrumental in building up Wendell Willkie as the nominee in 1940," John Cowles said. "Ike told me that Nixon should not be the 1960 nominee. 'You must stop Nixon,' the President said.

" 'Stop him with whom?' I asked. Then, to show you how politically naive Ike was, he suggested Bob Anderson, secretary of the Treasury, as a good possibility."

Cowles said he replied: "You can't be serious, Mr. President." There was no possible way to build Robert Anderson into a formidable candidate, John Cowles said.

Later, Eisenhower again asked John to come to the White House and talk politics. Again Ike urged Cowles to try to defeat Nixon in the 1960 GOP convention. This time, Cowles said, "Ike suggested Harold Stassen as a possibility." Once again, John Cowles said, he told the President that stopping Nixon was highly improbable. (On neither occasion did Eisenhower spell out why he did not favor Nixon as the party's presidential candidate.)

How well did Eisenhower perform in the White House? "I think he showed good common sense," John Cowles said. "He didn't get us involved in war. But I think John Foster Dulles was a hell of a poor secretary of state. . . .

"Ike generally was an honest, limited fellow. Fifty years from now I think they will say Ike was a kindly, benevolent, honorable, honest man, but he certainly wasn't a great president, like Truman, for example, who will go down as one of the great presidents."

In his post-retirement interview, John Cowles classified himself politically "not as a Republican really, but an independent with Democratic leanings." The Republican party, he said, has gone "ultraconservative while I've become more liberal as I learned more."

Which of the outstanding world figures he has met has

impressed him most? "I think Paul Hoffman may have been the greatest man I have ever known well," he said. "I went around the world twice with him. He is a completely dedicated and honorable individual, very competent, a wonderful salesman who gets along with everybody — a wonderful fellow."

Cowles called Winston Churchill "a great and magnificent leader in a critical time in England, with outstanding eloquence, vigor and courage .... But I would not rate him in character nearly as highly as Hoffman."

Across the years, John Cowles's focus, however much he traveled and whichever leader he met, remained upon the quality of the Cowles newspapers. As John Cowles approached the end of his active career, a Minneapolis friend summed him up:

"John Cowles believes newspapers should be a nation's greatest educational force, a university at the doorstep. When I think of John, a picture comes to mind. He had just returned [to Minneapolis] from India, aghast at [Prime Minister Jawaharlal] Nehru's problems.

"Two days later, every big wheel in the city — business, labor, editors, clergy — was seated in a Minneapolis club, before a huge map of Asia. And there, lecturing earnestly, pointer in hand, was John Cowles."

American journalism has changed during the more than 70 years since Gardner Cowles and Harvey Ingham moved to Des Moines from Algona. John Cowles, one of the heirs to the Cowles-Ingham "sense of mission" brand of journalism, has summed up some of the consequences of those changes. In 1954, when he was honorary president of Sigma Delta Chi, the journalists' fraternity, he found more good than bad in monopoly newspapering in a speech before the group's national convention in Columbus, Ohio.

"The best papers in America do not have a paper competing with them in their morning or evening local field. [They are] the most responsibly edited, the fairest, the most complete, the most accurate and objective." Such financially sound papers, he said, also are "better able to resist the pressure to sensationalize the news, to play up the cheap sex story, to headline the story that will sell the most copies rather than another story that may be of far more importance and significance."

John Cowles's argument that editors and publishers in non-competitive fields can have "a deeper feeling of their responsibilities and obligations to their communities and readers because of the very absence of competition" is illustrated by the papers that the Gardner Cowles-Harvey Ingham tradition fathered in both Des Moines and Minneapolis.

John Cowles discovered that in his professional lifetime newspapers' performance and quality have improved "enormously." Newspapers, he told his Columbus audience, have become "generally more responsible. Their news handling has become fairer, more objective and more complete. . . . No longer is there a 'kept' press of any significance, whether party organs designed to advance the interest of some political boss or mouthpieces intended to protect the economic interests of some public utility. People soon sense whether or not a newspaper is being edited in the public interest."

HARVEY INGHAM

GARDNER COWLES

SCENES from the offices of the **Register** and **Leader,** 1905.

THE HOME of The
Des Moines Register
and Evening Tribune
in 1915 at Fourth
and Court streets
This building was
abandoned for the
thirteen story struc-
ture which The Reg-
ister and Tribune
plant now occupies
on Eighth and Locust
streets.

EARLY HOME (above left) of **The Des Moines Register** and **Tribune** at Fourth Street and Court Avenue. It was abandoned for the 13 story structure (above right) on Eighth and Locust. In 1961 the exterior was remodeled as shown below.

PORTRAIT of Gardner Cowles and his sons in their early Des Moines years. (left to right) John, Russell, Gardner, sr. and Gardner (Mike), jr.

TRAVELERS, Gardner Cowles, sr. and his wife Florence in 1924 trekked to Egypt, with its views of pyramids and sphinx.

NOW LOOK PLEASANT, PLEASE!

"DING" BEGINS HIS WORK OF CARTOONING DES MOINES.
Commencing tomorrow his cartoons will be a daily feature of The Register and Leader.

JAY NORWOOD DARLING, long time **Register** editorial cartoonist. Ding's first cartoon (above) for **The Register** in 1906 upset local clergymen.

IN GOOD OLD U. S. A.

AN ORPHAN AT 8 IS NOW ONE OF THE WORLD'S GREATEST MINING ENGINEERS AND ECONOMISTS WHOSE AMBITION IS TO ELIMINATE THE CYCLE OF DEPRESSION AND UNEMPLOYMENT

THE SON OF A PLASTERER IS NOW THE WORLD'S GREATEST NEUROLOGIST AND HIS HOBBY IS GOOD HEALTH FOR POOR CHILDREN

A PRINTER'S APPRENTICE IS NOW CHIEF EXECUTIVE OF THE UNITED STATES

DRAWN IN 1923 BY J.N. DARLING AND AWARDED THE PULITZER PRIZE FOR THE BEST U.S CARTOON OF THE YEAR—

BUT THEY DIDN'T GET THERE BY HANGING AROUND THE CORNER DRUG STORE

IN THE GOOD OLD U.S.A. won the 1924 Pulitzer Prize for editorial cartooning for J. N. Darling.

WILLIAM WESLEY WAYMACK, editorial page editor and 1938 Pulitzer Prize winner.

MIKE COWLES in 1921 at his graduation from Phillips Exeter Academy.

THE NEW GENERATION: Gardner (Mike) Cowles, jr. and John Cowles in the mid-1930s.

QUESTERS FOR QUALITY. Editor Harvey Ingham and Publisher Gardner Cowles, sr. in 1937.

HARVEY INGHAM
at his desk
as usual on his
sixtieth anniver-
sary as a news-
paper editor.

What a Place For a Waste Paper Salvage Campaign.

DING's Pulitzer Prize winner for 1943.

RETIREMENT PARTY. Gardner Cowles, jr. and Kenneth MacDonald in January 1977 at MacDonald's retirement as editorial chairman after 50 years with **The Register** and **Tribune.**

9 MIKE COWLES

Like his father before him, Gardner Cowles, jr. — Mike Cowles — believed in trusting his employees. When he retired as president of the company in 1973, a *Register* editorial reiterated a view of him often expressed by his employees. It said: "He never has been a man to look over your shoulder. He believes in attracting competent people and giving them room to work."

For an editor, making that kind of room means handling fairly frequent demands and requests to suppress stories about advertisers and newsmakers who would rather avoid public attention. Mike Cowles's consistent answer to those pressures was like that of subsequent editors: He would not interfere with a trusted reporter writing a legitimate news story no matter how much advertising revenue was involved.

Mike Cowles worked summers as a reporter while he was a Harvard student, then joined the *Tribune* staff full-time in 1925 after graduation. In succeeding years, he served as city editor of *The Register,* assistant managing editor, managing editor, executive editor, associate publisher, president of the company and chairman of the board. He also launched *Look, Quick, Flair* and *Venture* magazines.

Even when he was a youngster, Mike Cowles spent a great deal of time at the newspaper office. "As a 5- and 6-year-old kid, I used to enjoy being in the cashier's cage," he said. "In those days, the newspapers paid the employees in metal coins. The lower-echelon people got paid in silver dollars, the better-paid ones in five-dollar gold pieces. My father made up the payroll himself. He put the money into manilla envelopes." At age 8, Mike Cowles was paid 25 cents for reading editorials — and thought the pay was too low. He attended Phillips Exeter Academy during World

War I and became editor of the weekly student paper, *The Exonian,* like his brother John before him. At Harvard, he edited *The Crimson,* of which his brother also had been editor.

In Des Moines, he was no armchair executive. He frequently roamed the world to satisfy an insatiable curiosity and to talk with great men about great issues. He interviewed Winston Churchill, Josef Stalin, Chiang Kai-shek and Nikita Khrushchev. At the personal urging of President Franklin D. Roosevelt, Mike Cowles took command of the domestic division of the U.S. Office of War Information (OWI) during World War II. He helped direct the 1940 campaign of Wendell Willkie and the 1952 campaign of Dwight Eisenhower for the Republican presidential nominations in those years, and he helped Willkie get "One World," his famous, best-selling book on postwar international co-operation, ready for publication.

Though the Cowles papers stressed keeping their political preferences on the editorial page, that policy did not inhibit the Cowles sons' personal efforts on behalf of Willkie. It is conceivable that Willkie never would have received the 1940 Republican presidential nomination without the advice and strenuous effort of John and Mike Cowles. Though his beginnings as a candidate are not directly connected to a history of the *Register* growth under the leadership of Gardner Cowles and Harvey Ingham, the Willkie-Cowles brothers story illustrates the papers' practice and policy versus its publishers' political predilections. Reporters and editors could hardly fail to note the Cowles brothers' interest in Willkie, but the story was generally treated according to standard rules. Any Willkie story had to take its chances and be weighed for relative newsworthiness against competing stories on any news day.

Mike and John Cowles met Willkie, president of Commonwealth and Southern Corp., in April of 1940, when he was a very dark horse indeed in the GOP-nomination race, being led at that point by Senators Robert A. Taft of Ohio and Arthur Vandenberg of Michigan and New York Gov. Thomas E. Dewey. (Russell Davenport of *Fortune* magazine, who had begun promoting Willkie for the presidency, introduced him to the Cowles brothers at a dinner in New York.)

"Willkie expressed interest in running," Mike Cowles said. "He said that all he wanted to do was to get himself well known on the eastern seaboard, and, if there appeared to be a deadlock in the convention, he might be the dark-horse nominee.

"My brother John and I told him he was nuts. If none of the delegates knew him except those on the eastern seaboard, they would be afraid to go for him, a Wall Street tycoon earning $100,000 a year as head of a utility company. Roosevelt was attacking hell out of utility companies."

The Cowles brothers suggested that Willkie come to St. Paul, Minn., and Des Moines on a trial-balloon trip on which he could become acquainted with as many GOP convention delegates as possible. Willkie had a great deal of ground to cover, because he had problems that included the fact that he had called himself a Democrat as late as 1938 and had not registered as a Republican until 1939.

Willkie made his first appearance before 80 or 100 persons in a St. Paul hotel ballroom by reading a speech.

"It was no good, " Mike Cowles said. "He never did learn to read a speech. He just couldn't. John bought radio time around Minnesota for the occasion. When Willkie finished, he knew he had been a flop. When he heard the announcer at the end of the banquet table say: 'We now return you to the studio,' Wendell took the speech and flung it into the air. The sheets just fluttered all over hell's half-acre.

"It was a two-story ballroom and it was a hot night. Willkie took off his coat and shouted: 'Now that I'm off the air, I'm going to tell you what I really think of the Roosevelt administration!' And he went up and down that platform snorting and yelling for at least another 25 minutes, and when he finished, that crowd got up on their chairs and screamed and yelled their applause."

Then and there, Mike said, Willkie gained the support of half a dozen national convention delegates.

A few nights later, Willkie came to Des Moines, where, Mike said, "I told him he couldn't read a speech." Thirty-five hundred persons turned out to hear Willkie in KRNT Theater. Paying no attention to the available microphone, he paced back and forth across the wide stage, speaking in a ringing and rasping voice and stirring the crowd with his castigation of the New Deal. Again, he was a big hit.

Though *The Register* covered Willkie's activities gener-ously before and after the speech, the speech story itself barely made Page One because of the disastrous war news. Advancing Nazi troops were plunging through France in the heyday of their blitzkrieg. The Willkie speech story was limited to a one-column headline on Page One, with a couple of leading paragraphs that were repeated on an inside page layout that included a display of pictures and considerable type.

As Willkie's appeal grew, top national magazines started going hell-bent for his candidacy. Henry Luce, publisher of *Time, Life* and *Fortune,* gave him strong support from his drive's early days. Mike Cowles put Willkie's picture on the cover of his *Look* magazine right before the late-June Republican convention in Philadelphia.

Both Mike and John Cowles spent much time working for Willkie, rallying prominent bankers and lawyers and other Willkie supporters to concentrate on trying to convert delegates to the man from Elwood, Indiana. Said Mike Cowles: "The pace just about killed me. I flew over dozens of states with Willkie to meet delegates. By the time the convention opened, he had met about two-thirds of the delegates." The brothers "did a hell of a lot of things," John Cowles said, "but I don't mean we were alone. There were lots of other people doing things."

At the tumultuous convention, Willkie won the nomination on the sixth ballot, an outcome that John Cowles called "a one-in-a-million miracle shot."

It *was* a miracle of sorts for a recent Democratic liberal to smash the regular Republican organizations with the blitz campaign for the nomination, but "miracle" is far from the full explanation. Willkie, a big bear of a man with magnetism and courage, proved to have strong appeal to the people in the spring of 1940. Newspaper and magazine coverage helped build him into a powerful political force that smothered the oldtime politicians.

The people in the galleries at Philadelphia reflected this deep-seated public feeling with insistent chants of "We want Willkie. We want Willkie" that went out over the air to the remotest corners of the country.

The Willkie hotel room scene when word came of the nomination was unforgettable, Mike Cowles said. "Wendell used to wear a hard-brimmed straw hat," he said. "He had been listening to the radio in his hotel room. The rest of us were in the adjoining sitting room. When the final vote came, I ran into the bedroom to congratulate him.

"Willkie had his hat tilted over one eye. He was strutting back and forth, looking at himself in the mirror. He was pleased with himself for pulling it off."

An innovator and trailblazer in the communications field,

Mike Cowles during his early years of authority at *The Register* and *The Tribune* greatly strengthened sports coverage, was instrumental in the company decision to use aircraft in covering Iowa stories and helped exploit the advantages of news pictures when the Associated Press began its picture transmission by Wirephoto, which gave the papers great competitive advantage in using timely photographs.

In 1926, when he took over as city editor of *The Register,* he displayed fairness and "a lot of competence," one veteran reporter said. Mike Cowles also assumed an increasing share of leadership in the news department generally.

"That was when we beefed up the sports sections," Cowles himself said. Like Managing Editor Bill Waymack and Circulation Manager Bill Cordingley, the newest Cowles in the business was sports-minded. With Mike Cowles in the forefront, the sports section grew to 10 pages in *The Sunday Register* during football seasons. Few, if any, other papers could boast of such sports coverage at the time. After the papers acquired their own plane in 1928, the sports department embarked on the then-spectacular practice of flying photographers and reporters all over the Midwest for fast picture-and-story coverage of major football games. *Sunday Register* circulation moved steadily upward, but there were doubts whether the gains justified the sharply higher expenses. Mike admitted that the enterprise was costly but, he said, "We're having a helluva lot of fun."

Other sections merited his attention, too. Characteristic of his approach was a speech in 1936 before the American Society of Newspaper Editors in which he said he would like to add "a good Socialist writer to *The Register* [as an editorial page columnist] if I could find one who writes vigorously." Like Harvey Ingham and Gardner Cowles, sr., Mike Cowles wanted the editorial page to be provocative and a forum for all shades of opinion.

One of Mike Cowles's most interesting contributions to the field of communications had to do with readership surveys. He hired George Gallup, who was studying for a doctorate at the University of Iowa, to do some surveys on what Iowans liked to read in *The Sunday Register*. Gallup said he found that he received pretty much the same opinions from surveying a small group of selected readers as from a larger number. He asked himself: Why not just talk to a carefully chosen cross-section and save money? Thus was born his method of sample polling. Gallup went on to found the American Institute of Public Opinion, which conducts the Gallup Poll.

Gallup also discovered in his polling for *The Register* that the highest readership in a newspaper went not to the printed word but to the printed word *plus* related pictures and especially sequence pictures.

Using the survey results, Mike Cowles greatly expanded picture usage in the Des Moines papers. A 1937 survey showed that *The Des Moines Tribune* carried more photographs in a six-day period than 51 other leading newspapers in the country. Second was *The New York Mirror,* third *The Chicago Times,* fourth *The Des Moines Register,* fifth *The New York World-Telegram* and sixth *The New York News.*

Mike Cowles was credited with helping create the new picture journalism and with originating the serial picture rotogravure idea, which was spreading across the country. The picture-series stories in *The Register*'s roto section fascinated Iowa readers and became one of several reasons for the phenomenal growth of the Sunday paper's circulation in the Great Depression. Sometimes a layout consisted only of two pictures; at other times a half-dozen or more photographs were displayed on an entire page. Each picture carried brief explanatory material.

The picture coverage delighted other newspaper audiences as well and the Register and Tribune Syndicate was able to sell photo features to papers around the country.

Sales were so good that Mike Cowles in 1936 decided to start a national picture magazine, to be named *Look.* The new publication was about to be established when Cowles learned that another national picture magazine, to be named *Life,* was to be launched by the publishers of *Time* magazine. Mike and John Cowles were on friendly terms with Henry Luce and Roy Larsen, top officials of *Time,* and so the four met to talk over the situation. By exchanging experimental dummies of their proposed magazines, they discovered that their approaches were going to be different. *Life* planned to be a weekly *news* picture magazine, *Look* a monthly geared mainly to *feature* photographs.

The Cowleses decided to wait and see what happened to *Life.* It was an immediate success on its appearance in

November of 1936. *Look* was launched Jan. 5, 1937 (subscription price $1 for 12 issues) and also was immediately successful.

Introducing the new magazine, Mike Cowles wrote: "Iowa readers of *Look* will recognize some of the same picture techniques which have been used so successfully in *The Sunday Register* rotogravure section during the past year, the technique of using unusual continuity picture stories rather than unrelated news pictures."

Look did not remain a monthly for long. Encouraged by the initial response, the sale of 705,000 copies of the first issue and more than one million for the second, Mike in April of 1937 switched to publishing the magazine every other Tuesday. Initial issues were criticized as "sensationalist," but the critics changed their attitude before the magazine's first year was out. In October of 1937, *The New Republic*, which had disparaged *Look* as "morgue and dime museum on paper" months before, commended the magazine for carrying "the best pictorial study of civil liberties in the United States we have seen anywhere."

Look's all-time peak circulation, 9.5 million copies, was reached in 1967 with the publication of four installments from the book "The Death of a President," William Manchester's account of the assassination of John Fitzgerald Kennedy.

Like his brother John, Mike Cowles traveled abroad with Wendell Willkie. Shortly after Cowles was named head of the domestic news section of the Office of War Information, he traveled with Willkie on a fact-finding trip to Russia, the Middle East and China. Willkie's mission, set up by President Roosevelt, aimed at bolstering Allied morale in the dark early days of World War II and at encouraging neutrals not to yield to Nazi pressure.

The 50-day trip held dangers that today's jet travelers do not know. "People forget that in 1942 there was no airplane that had the range to cross the Atlantic," Mike Cowles said. "We flew down to Miami, to Puerto Rico and then down to Belem, a town out on the hump of Brazil, the part of South America that is closest to Africa.

"We next flew from Belem to Accra in West Africa. I'll never forget when we first saw land ahead. [Later] the pilot came to us greatly relieved. He had had only 18 minutes of fuel left."

The flight continued across Africa to Khartoum. "We flew down the Nile to Cairo," Cowles said. "We arrived two weeks before the crucial battle of El Alamein. We went out into the desert and spent a night in the tent of General [Bernard Law] Montgomery, [commander of the British forces]. He gave us a two-hour briefing on how he was going to whip [German Field Marshal Erwin] Rommel."

In a stopover in Ankara, Turkey, Mike said, Willkie "did one great job" talking the Turks out of joining the German side of the war. The party continued to Moscow, where Willkie conferred with Josef Stalin, across the whole of Russia, to Chungking, China, and talks with Nationalist leader Chiang Kai-shek and then on to Alaska and to the U.S. mainland.

While in Chungking, Willkie issued a statement saying he found four major sentiments in the countries he visited: They wanted the Allies to win, they wanted the Allies to take the offensive, they wanted an end to colonialism after the war and they shared doubts of varying degrees about the readiness of "the leading democracies of the world to stand up and be counted for freedom for others after the war is over."

Willkie emphasized the necessity for ending colonialism. "No foot of Chinese soil, for example, should be or can be ruled from now on except by the people who live on it," he said.

The Register agreed editorially: "We must really be for a free world. And it must include progressive realization of economic freedom. . . . The war is global. Peace must be global. The world must be . . . organized for the deliberate purpose of producing rising standards of living for all, as well as political liberty in such forms as people want it. Exploitation of nation by nation . . . has got to be 'out the window.' "

Twenty years later, in the same Kremlin room where Willkie and Cowles met Stalin, Cowles had an exclusive three-hour interview with Soviet Premier Nikita Khrushchev. In the 1962 interview, Cowles felt Khrushchev "wanted to leave a good impression with us and hoped it would be conveyed to the American public." Khrushchev also was cordial toward *The Register,* which had played a key role in clearing the way for a Russian farm delegation to come to Iowa to study American agriculture's efficient methods. (In 1956, Lauren Soth, chief editorial writer for the Cowles papers in Des Moines, had won a Pulitzer Prize for the editorial that led to the breakthrough in establishing good agricultural relations between the United States and the Soviet Union.)

The 1962 interview was cordial, unlike an earlier confrontation between Mike Cowles and Nikita Khrushchev. In 1959, while on an American tour, Khrushchev addressed the Economic Club of New York and said, among other things that he wanted Americans and Russians to become better acquainted. In response, Mike Cowles rose to make a point about freedom of the press and freedom of information. He said:

"That being your feeling, why is it, sir, that you will not allow your people, if they wish, to listen to a broadcast from the United States, and why is it that you do not allow periodicals, magazines and newspapers to be distributed freely throughout the Soviet Union, and why is it that when the Soviet journalists resident in the U.S. are allowed to send any dispatches they want without any interference from the government or anybody else, why do you insist on censoring the dispatches of American correspondents in the Soviet Union?"

Khrushchev, replying through an interpreter, said the circumstances of the American invitation for his visit included an agreement "that our discussions will not bear on the affairs of either country."

When members of the audience cried out, "Answer the question!" Khrushchev replied, with some irritation:

"I am an old sparrow, so as to say, and you cannot muddle me with your cries. . . . I come here as a representative of a great country, a great people who have made a great revolution, and no cries can deafen, can do away with the great achievements of our people."

Again there were shouts of "Answer the question!"

To that, Khrushchev said:

"I will reply to the question when there are no interruptions. The reply is this: The question of what is listened to or read should be decided, not by any outside government or any outside influence but by our own people and by the government."

Khrushchev never did give a satisfactory explanation as to why the Russians jammed American radio broadcasts, why American publications were banned from the Soviet Union, or why American reporters were not permitted to file uncensored news reports from Russia.

Later, the official Soviet news agency, Tass, called Mike

Cowles's challenge "provocative" and termed *Look* a "notorious" magazine.

"Provocative" or not, the questions had at least been asked.

However occupied he was elsewhere, in New York or Washington, D. C., or overseas, Mike Cowles kept a close eye on the Des Moines newspaper operation and remained active in making news and editorial policy.

His newspaper philosophy grew out of his Des Moines background. In 1955, he told an audience of educators at Simpson College at Indianola, Iowa, that "the greatest editors I know are just like the greatest educators and are successful for the same reason. They are thoughtful men with scrupulous regard for the truth. They are men who strive to stir the best in the human race, not pander to the worst. They are men of courage who dare to lead, even when the direction is temporarily dangerous and unpopular."

Perhaps recalling Harvey Ingham, he said the best editors "are men who see the world whole, who know that mankind is capable of mounting to the sublime, as Winston Churchill said, if someone will fire the imagination and sketch a vision." The public, Mike Cowles said, "is astoundingly quick to sense whether it should trust the men running a particular magazine or particular newspaper or radio network."

"This reputation for trust or confidence is the most priceless ingredient any medium can have," he told the educators. "I have often said we will have more good newspapers and magazines when more of them are headed by better men. It is as simple as that. We are both, you educators and I, in the most exciting business in the world — that of helping our fellow men learn better ways to communicate with each other, of helping them to understand and to find the useful and the good life."

In a 1966 speech, he expanded upon the "public character" of newspapers, declaring that they "not only inform and entertain. They are invested with responsibility for truth, fairness and balance, completeness and newness, coupled with their responsibility as the monitor and conscience of their community and nation."

When Mike Cowles at age 70 ended his active career with the Register and Tribune Company, the farewell editorial written by then-Editor Kenneth MacDonald cited Mike Cowles's penchant for constantly probing, searching, experimenting: "He recognized, long before best-sellers were written about it, that change is a constant fact of life, and that any organization — a city, a state, a newspaper — must be willing to experiment with new ideas if it is to remain alive and healthy . . . ."

One other quality, one among many that he acquired from his father, also stood him in good stead. Like the elder Cowles, he could cut his losses and rise above discouraging developments. "I try never to look back and never to regret any decision," he said. "There is no point in it. The only way to get fun out of life is to look ahead."

10 NEWSPAPER PEOPLE

Distinctive personalities who also have writing, editing, drawing or camera talent are the stuff of an excellent newspaper. *The Register* has had its share of free spirits, inventive editors and competitive newsmen.

For decades, primary among the first-rank personalities at *The Register* was Jay Norwood (Ding) Darling, the paper's editorial cartoonist from 1906 to 1949 except for two hiatuses. He had the fine cartoonist's gift for summing up situations with fresh insight — whether the topic was politics or conservation. He coupled his talents to the free rein that Cowles and Ingham's regime gave him.

Like many of the top people Gardner Cowles and Harvey Ingham hired, Jay Darling was recruited from another Iowa paper — *The Sioux City Journal*. Darling, an amateur artist who had been making sketches around Sioux City as a hobby, was a 24-year-old reporter covering a trial when an irascible old lawyer swatted a rival attorney with his cane in the courtroom. Ding went back to his office, "wrote a big sensational story about it," and then got orders from his editor to go back and get a picture of the combative attorney, named Treadway.

"I found him still in the courtroom and secretly pointed the camera at him," Darling said, "that is, I thought I was doing it secretly, but he caught sight of me." Treadway "let out a war whoop" and chased Darling out of the courtroom and down a flight of stairs, swinging his cane and missing him but "stirring up a breeze" at the back of the reporter's neck.

Crestfallen at missing the photograph, Darling offered "a sort of sketch I made of the old fellow the other day." The sketch caught the Treadway personality, the editor ran it on Page One, and Darling's sketches of various citizens became a daily *Journal* feature.

"That's how I became a cartoonist," Darling said. "They paid me more for making a sketch every day than for running around on my feet all day reporting."

Like others on the paper, Darling was the son of a clergyman, a Congregational minister who used the abbreviation D'ng for his last name. Two of his sons, including Jay Darling, used the same abbreviation and eventually printers converted "D'ng" to "Ding." The family moved from Michigan to Sioux City when Jay Darling was a boy and he began sketching when he was eight years old, copying a humorous drawing of two Irishmen on a picture postcard that a family friend had sent from London.

Darling moved to the Des Moines job in 1906 — and his first cartoon for *The Register* got him into trouble. Irritated by the heavy pall of smoke usually visible over Des Moines, he drew a cartoon based on one version of the derivation of the city's name — that "Des Moines" stemmed from the French word for "monk." Darling drew a picture of a fat monk smoking a pipe from which smoke was billowing. The monk, of course, was labeled "Des Moines," and the pipe bowl bore the words "soft coal."

Catholics were angered at a cartoon some of them regarded as neither sympathetic nor dignified. Darling "learned not to use the garb of a priest or monk in cartoons, although I meant no reflection on the church or the dignity of the cloth. . . ."

Whatever hard feelings there were evaporated quickly, and the energetic and good-looking Darling was soon popular around Des Moines. He was notable for, among other things, eating pie for breakfast and singing baritone in the Plymouth Congregational Church choir.

In Darling's maturity, when he was 56, a national magazine writer described him in a 1933 article as "a tall (six feet), husky, friendly-looking man, with horn-rimmed specs perched comfortably on his nose, cigarette in a holder cocked up from the corner of his mouth, and pencil running swiftly and deftly under his strong fingers." He was a complex man — stern and warm, contentious and agreeable by turns.

The reason for Darling's quitting *The Register* in 1911 has been forgotten — perhaps it was a matter of one of his strong-minded disagreements with management — but in any case he went east to work for the old *New York Globe* and other papers linked in a syndicate. To the dismay of *Register* editors, Darling's syndicated cartoons began appearing on Page One of the rival *Des Moines Capital.*

The dismay did not last long. In 1913, less than two years after leaving, Darling returned to Des Moines and *The Register,* explaining that in New York he could not keep contact with people or nature. He also wanted complete independence in his work and found that he "could not be that kind of a cartoonist" in New York. One of his complaints was that his Manhattan editors wanted him to draw comic strips, which he refused to do.

The Register welcomed Darling back with open pages — the first Sunday he resumed working for the paper, Ding cartoons of the past were scattered all through the paper and a full page was given to his sketches, under the headline: "J. N. Darling, That's Ding, Comes Back."

Despite repeated efforts by big Eastern papers to lure Darling away from Des Moines again, he always came to the same conclusion: He would stay with *The Register.* His reputation was such that *The Kansas City Star* said at the time: "There are a lot of folks who consider Jay Norwood Darling the best cartoonist in this broad land at present. The publishers of a large number of newspapers much bigger and more influential than *The Des Moines Register* are numbered among the people who entertain such thoughts. . . . Everybody in Des Moines knows that Ding is getting far less money than he could if he would only consent to go East."

Darling once talked in metaphor about his preference for living in Iowa: "Out west we have to get our seafood canned. But rather canned seafood and fresh friendships than canned friendships and fresh seafood! When you boil all the superfluous water out of life, and sugar off, if you haven't gathered a goodly residue of friendships and affections, you aren't going to have much sweetness left in the kettle." In 1928, he said: "By staying in Iowa, I can get closer to the real thoughts of the people and closer to my friends than in the great cities. Moreover, the Middle West is more purely American than is the East."

His love of the outdoors and his fondness for hunting and fishing no doubt also were important reasons why he preferred the wide open spaces beyond the Mississippi to the East's big cities.

Jay Darling did not regard himself as a gifted artist — he habitually drove editors to distraction by fiddling with his drawings up to and past deadline, often trying to redraw an entire cartoon. His theory was that "cartooning is not an art; you need not be talented to do it." He contended that "any boy with an average amount of intelligence who will carry around a pad of paper and a pencil with him all the time, making five or six sketches a day from life, will, in five years, have acquired enough skill to take a minor position as a cartoonist. His success after that will not be slow in coming if he works hard."

Darling was so certain of his theory that he bet Editor Ingham that he could train Harold (Tom) Carlisle — a University of Iowa taxidermy student who planned to be an explorer, but who also had been doing some drawing at the U of I — to become a more-than-competent cartoonist. The cartoonist was so successful with Carlisle that when Darling retired his prize student wound up as cartoonist for *The Register*.

Darling consistently warned students that drawing is the smallest part of the cartoonist's task, that getting an idea is the major requirement. Darling, who in later years read six daily newspapers, advised: "You must read at least two good newspapers a day, especially the international and national news, the state news and always the editorials. Your knowledge of world events will grow along with your ability to sketch as you keep on practicing. . . . Most people think a cartoonist just sits around in his bedroom slippers and lounging robe, waiting for an inspiration. . . . I'm sorry, but that isn't the way it is."

In the back of his mind was an always-present worry that he might fail to come up with good cartoon ideas. Advising apprentice cartoonists, he said: "If you have to make a cartoon every day, you will do well to have several barrels of sour mash fermenting on the side to be ready to use if the particular batch you planned to use for the day doesn't cook. You will need a lot of yeast and I don't know any drugstore where it can be bought. You have to make your own. Then all you have to do is draw it."

The quality of his drawing bothered him always, no more so than on the day in 1942 to commemorate the first anniversary of the Japanese sneak attack on Pearl Harbor. Titled "Remember," the drawing pictured an angry Uncle Sam holding a dead sailor who had been stabbed in the back. In subordinate positions were an advancing American Army and American planes.

Darling did not finish the penciled drawing until the last afternoon before the deadline for printing the color cartoon in *The Register*. He asked Managing Editor Kenneth MacDonald what he thought of it. "Looks great to me," said MacDonald, who then asked how long it would take Darling to get the color ready.

Looking at the sketch from different angles, the cartoonist muttered: "I don't think it looks quite right." Then, to MacDonald's horror, Darling picked up a piece of art gum as "big as a baseball" and began to erase the drawing. Darling worked for hours on a new drawing, and got it completed for the second time, still before the deadline, and the cartoon ran as scheduled.

"The original drawing just didn't measure up to what Ding wanted," MacDonald said. "The second sketch was identical with the first so far as I could tell. But he wasn't quite satisfied. He was tremendously conscientious."

Darling was habitually late with his drawings not only because of drawing problems but also because he wanted to be as up-to-date as possible with late-breaking news. "The first thing I observed about Ding was how hard he worked," MacDonald said. "Everyone knows he had a great talent. . . . Yet the more I came to know him the more I realized that his working habits, his great concentration, the exacting standards he set for himself were probably more responsible for his success than his talent. He was always drawing, or observing, or preparing to draw. His talent was great, but in my judgment his industry was greater."

On the subject of judgment, Darling once observed that it is hard to find an editor "who knows the difference between a good and a poor cartoon." He added wryly: "I will admit that I have never been quite sure myself."

Another of Darling's cliffhanger situations involved what became perhaps the best-known Ding cartoon. The technicians were up against the cartoon deadline, so Darling picked up a discarded sketch from the floor of his studio in the Register and Tribune Building, and told them to use it in the first edition, that he would have another ready later. Though he wasn't much pleased with the drawing — and neither were *Register* editors — he couldn't come up with a better one, and so "The Long, Long Trail" ran through all editions.

It was Darling's tribute to a fellow outdoorsman and con-servationist, Theodore Roosevelt, former president of the United States, who died Jan. 6, 1919. It pictured a shadowy Roosevelt on horseback, waving good-by with his campaign hat as he joined a procession of departed American pioneers winding in covered wagons into the distant past.

In New York, editors of the *The Herald-Tribune* were cool to the drawing and didn't print it immediately. But the editors and Darling were wrong about the effectiveness of "The Long, Long Trail." His tribute was received with a feeling of reverence for Roosevelt as a beloved figure; the drawing ran in more than 100 newspapers that used Ding cartoons. (His drawings were distributed by the New York Herald-Tribune Syndicate from 1917 to 1949.)

Darling was never happy with the sketch, believing it was too much like one he drew in 1917 upon the death of Iowa-born William F. (Buffalo Bill) Cody, plainsman and Indian fighter. Few readers were aware of the similarity, or if they were it didn't matter. "It probably was the most exalted drawing Ding ever made," said Mark Sullivan, Washington columnist and author.

Darling's 1924 Pulitzer Prize cartoon showed how an orphan at 10 grew up to become a great mining engineer and economist, noted for helping to feed starving nations after World War I (Herbert Hoover), how a printer's ap-prentice became president in later life (Warren G. Harding) and how a plasterer's son became a great neurol-ogist (not identified). The caption said: "But they didn't get there hanging around the corner drugstore." Darling won the 1943 Pulitzer for a cartoon picturing wartime Washing-ton, D. C., buried under piles of government reports and bulletins. The caption said: "What a Place for a Waste Paper Salvage Campaign."

Darling did not think the 1943 cartoon deserved the award. He told a colleague that the point was not plain, the cartoon was not well-drawn and the idea constituted criticism of the government in wartime, which he really did not like to do. Years afterward, he said of the Pulitzer Prize selection committee to a friend: "I think those dimwits must have spread out a lot of cartoons and then decided the winner by saying: 'Eeny, meeny, miney, mo.' "

Jay Darling was a favorite cartoonist of every president from Theodore Roosevelt to Harry Truman. President Franklin D. Roosevelt asked for, and received, many Ding originals, but Mrs. Roosevelt never forgave Darling for once depicting her husband as Little Lord Fauntleroy. President Herbert Hoover, a friend, was on the mailing list for copies of all Ding cartoons while Hoover was in the White House and he also received a stack of original sketches.

Although cartoons, because of their topicality, often are of ephemeral interest, several of Darling's special subjects almost guaranteed work of enduring value, beyond Ding's formula for the successful cartoon. Such a drawing, he said, should contain "a little medicine, a little sugar-coating and as much humor as the subject will bear."

Part of Darling's unrelenting battle for nature conservation resulted in his being called "the best friend wild ducks ever had." But his interests were broader than fish and game; he also assailed poor farming practices that were robbing the nation of valuable topsoil through erosion. One cartoon pictured "the equivalent of 125,000 farms of 160 acres each moving down the river."

He was equally exercised about industries' and cities' pollution of streams and lakes, and he attacked the "sight pollution" spawned by billboards lining highways.

The federal government in the 1930s set up programs not only to relieve drought conditions and prevent their recurrence but also to preserve wild game, whose numbers had declined precipitously in the bone-dry early 1930s. U.S. Agriculture Secretary Henry A. Wallace of Des Moines, a Democrat, in 1934 appointed Darling, a Republican, as head of the U.S. Biological Survey. Darling gave up a $100,000 annual income — much of it from his cartoon syndication — to take the federal job, which paid $8,000 a year.

One of Darling's first steps was to order a waterfowl survey; the report was that the number of ducks that had nested in the northern United States was less than 3 per cent of normal number. He embarked on an energetic federal program to provide more "living room" for waterfowl in the United States; 2,000 men worked to restore swamps and lakes that had been drained. Ultimately, in 20 months in the nation's capital, he secured $17 million in funds, which underwrote a plan that increased the number of federal game refuges from 33 to 220 and their total area from 700,000 acres to 5.7 million acres. Darling was called "the spark that set off that big explosion." In 1934, he also designed the first federal duck stamp — two ducks in flight — and in 1950 refused to allow his picture to be used on that year's stamp, contending that wildlife scenes should continue to be used on the stamps.

In his long career, Ding drew upward of 16,000 cartoons — and gave away some 10,000 of them in response to requests. Despite a pessimism that warred with the optimism that many of his cartoons displayed, he was happy to have lived when he did. When he was 84 years old, he wrote, in a characteristically two-sided comment:

"From where I sit, the view over a most remarkable period of history is both exciting and full of turbulent as well as happy memories. There hasn't been a dull moment.... Life has been nothing like so much as a perennial ride on a political and international roller coaster, with all its ups and downs and breathtaking curves."

At the same time, he doubted that he had accomplished very much: "I don't remember any political campaigns that have either been won or lost because of cartoons or cartoonists. I know of no general who won a war, no heathen who became a Christian and no candidate whose successes or failures were seriously altered by the use of cartoons. I don't think they ever moved any mountains or changed the course of history.... Even rabble-rousers among the cartoonists have never achieved great victories."

Sigma Delta Chi, the national journalism society, disagreed with Darling's pessimism in his old age. It designated the Register and Tribune Building as a "historic site" because of Darling's distinguished career as a cartoonist. In its citation, Sigma Delta Chi said Darling, using "a drawing board instead of a typewriter, became one of America's most influential and respected newspapermen in the first half of the Twentieth Century."

Jay Darling died Feb. 12, 1962, at the age of 85.

On the morning of Feb. 13, 1962, the last Ding cartoon appeared on Page One of *The Register*. It was headed: "Bye now - it's been wonderful knowing you." The sketch pictured his cluttered studio — discarded drawings on the floor, duck decoys and fishing rods behind the sofa, drawing board and artist's chair unoccupied — and the shadowy figure of Jay Darling disappearing out the door, waving his hat in farewell.

"We will never be able to measure the influence of Jay Darling," the *Register* editorial read. "All we know is that because of him millions of people have looked at the problems of our times from a fresh point of view, with sharper perspective, a new insight. And we know that influence of this type does not stop when today's paper is discarded. It goes on subtly into the future, its origin perhaps forgotten, but its force forever effective."

Like Jay Darling, William Wesley (Bill) Waymack was recruited to *The Register* from *The Sioux City Journal.* He joined the Cowles papers in 1918 as associate editor and an editorial writer. At *The Journal,* he had at one time or another filled nearly every job on the paper — church reporter, police reporter, court reporter, commercial editor, city hall reporter, night city editor and chief editorial writer. Twenty years later, when he was chief editorial writer for the Des Moines papers, he won the 1938 Pulitzer Prize for editorial writing.

He served as managing editor of *The Register* and *The Tribune* from 1921 to 1929 and took over in 1931 as editor of the editorial pages, where he made his greatest mark for the papers and the state's farm population, whose distress in the Twenties and Thirties heavily influenced the entire Iowa economy.

One of Waymack's greatest agricultural causes was the issue of "farm tenancy." The proportion of Iowa farmers tilling their own land had reached a low point; the issue was a grave one.

Renters farmed nearly six of every 10 Iowa acres in 1936. Thousands of farmers who lost ownership of their land in the Great Depression were forced to become renters. Mortgage foreclosures in the Twenties and Thirties turned 40,000 Iowa farm owners into tenants or forced them off their land. The cost was high in human terms; tenant families often had to live in rundown houses while hard-pressed landlords worried more about breaking even than about upkeep of dwellings. The economic price came high, too. Tenants moved a great deal — in 1935, some 37,000 farm-tenant families from among the state's 215,000 farms changed residences — and that moving often meant that renters worked the soil to exhaustion, knowing they would be elsewhere soon. Tenants usually moved to new homes on Mar. 1 each year, before the crop-planting season. Waymack called the massive "annual migration . . . a terrific economic waste, an enormous social loss." He concluded: "The tenant is the loser, the landlord is the loser, and the social soundness of Iowa is the loser."

Waymack sought to awaken the state and the country to the importance of conserving both farmers and farms with enlightened policies on tenancy. He called for reversing the trend down the "agricultural ladder" from ownership to tenancy, pointing out that the issue was an old one, "the accumulated result of generations of unthinking exploitation of our agricultural resources, both land and people."

His editorial eye fell on other distressed sections of the country as well. In 1936 he wrote that a national problem was developing in large American cities where many rural southerners were settling. He saw what that migration might do to a later generation.

In the South, Waymack wrote, "thanks to the Civil War, the race question, a vicious system of one-crop, cash-crop production ... we have a population of millions of low-grade farm tenants."

"They have a high birth rate. They include vast numbers of Negroes but [also] a large number of whites. Many of them are thoroughly incompetent, though they may come from the purest American stock. . . ."

"They are wage-slaves on the farm, working year after year to catch up with current debts to merchants and others, and never catching up. Their houses are often shanties. . . . They know nothing of sanitation. They have practically no educational opportunity."

Far from the southern fields, expressing the kind of national overview that had grown up in the Cowles-Ingham *Register,* he commented without mincing words: "Does any sane man think that conditions of that sort can go on forever without somehow affecting us? The future population of our cities is going to be drawn largely from those southern low castes. Our citizenry of tomorrow is in their seed."

Waymack was no drawing room farmer; in 1930, he bought a 275-acre tract along the Raccoon River 30 miles west of Des Moines and that became home base for the rest of his life. Others did the actual farming but Waymack enjoyed experimenting with crop techniques and the breeding of farm animals. Those close to the situation said he "practiced what he preached in owner-tenant relationships."

Waymack in 1937 received an honorable mention in the Pulitzer competition for the excellence of his editorials. A year later, his editorials on man and the land were instrumental in his winning the top prize; they are editorials that contain a sweep, a depth and a history-dominating quality as well as a sense of national prophecy. (The citation mentioned not only farm problems but also Waymack's editorials on industrial relations, political issues like F.D.R.'s Supreme Court-packing controversy, civil liberties, problems of democracy, foreign trade and international political relations.)

When President Roosevelt named Agriculture Secretary Henry A. Wallace to head a committee to study farm tenancy, Waymack became a member. That position undoubtedly insured that Wallace passed on to the president not only his own farm-tenancy ideas but Waymack's as well.

The *Register*'s news columns also carried a great deal of farm news, including the story of the passage of the 1937 farm-tenancy law, which provided for an experimental program of federal loans to tenants buying land. The program was modest, beginning with $10 million in federal funds the first year and continuing with $25 million the second and $50 million the third. By 1942, the Farm Security Administration program had assisted in 468 tenant-purchase loans in Iowa, not a large number, but then land purchases in 1937 already had shown sharp increases through regular channels. In 1937, the Iowa Legislature voted the homestead tax exemption law, designed to encourage home ownership by giving tax credit to families living in their own homes. The 1939 Legislature followed that up with a law that required a farm landlord to give notice not later than the preceding Nov. 1 if he planned to cancel a tenant's lease as of the following Mar. 1.

Waymack, a bespectacled, stocky man who liked sports and practical jokes, ranged across broad issues with a writing style "distinguished by force, clarity and directness." He supported and promoted the idea that editorial pages should present a wide range of views and he broadened the *Register*'s "Open Forum" letters-to-the-editor column because he considered that space for the expression of public opinion an important safety valve.

Named editor in 1943 upon Harvey Ingham's appointment as editor emeritus, Waymack served for three more years, then left the papers to become one of the original members of the Atomic Energy Commission. He left the AEC in 1948, returning to Des Moines, but did not return to the Register and Tribune Company. He died in 1960.

Waymack's focus on the farm situation was typical of one of the *Register*'s mainstays, its farm coverage. In the early 1920s, the paper sometimes carried two adjoining pages of farm news, but Gardner Cowles was not satisfied with the coverage even though it was extensive. Editorial writer Paul Appleby suggested as a candidate for farm editor J Stuart Russell, who had been Appleby's partner in publishing *The Sac County Bulletin,* a Sac City weekly paper. Russell had farmed five years near Newton after his graduation from Grinnell College in 1913 and knew his way around country newspapering from his five years' experience in Sac City.

Cowles hired Russell in 1925, warning him that the job would be permanent "only if you deliver." Russell delivered, becoming known all over the nation, and overseas as well, as a top-flight agricultural writer. (Around the newsroom, he was known as the man who fought a constant, losing battle over that initial J, which stood for nothing, even though he was often referred to as Jim.)

Russell helped expand the Cowles papers' coverage and took some lumps in the bargain. In 1932, when farmer protests over low prices were reaching their zenith in Iowa, Russell covered a meeting in Sioux City at which an estimated 5,000 farmers and their sympathizers (including some Communists, like North Dakota-based "Mother Bloor," Mrs. Andrew Omholt) were demanding better prices. Hundreds of the protesters surrounded the auto carrying photographer Maurice Horner and Russell, who was driving. By the time the uproar over the newsmen's presence had ended and the beating on the car and its occupants had subsided, Horner had been kicked by protesters and his camera had been smashed. Russell suffered blows on the head that left him unable to hear in his left ear for the rest of his life.

In 1937, as part of the *Register*'s interest in the farm-tenancy issue, Russell went south with a group of Midwestern farmers to see for themselves conditions in the cotton states. Russell's somberly dramatic *Register* story of what he found on the trip disconcerts the reader even now. The southern tenants, Russell wrote, lived in slums: "The fact that they are located in the country does not detract from the fact that their pitiful hovels lack every modern convenience.... Health and sanitary requirements are entirely ignored. Most Iowa farmers house their hogs in houses that present a better [outside] appearance...."

Russell was a gentle man, some might say too gentle for the hard-bitten business that newspapering often is. Serving as managing editor from 1943 to 1946 while Kenneth MacDonald served in the Navy, Russell brought a touch of camaraderie to the newsroom, combining that characteristic gentleness with the look of a big bear of a man (6 feet 2, 220 pounds).

He followed all the news, not just farm happenings, but his focus for the rest of his life was delving into farm problems as well as serving in a number of government posts. He remained a strong force and a vivid presence at *The Register* and *The Tribune* until his death in an automobile accident in 1960 at age 68.

A measure of what Russell meant to the staff personally as well as to the paper professionally is contained in former *Tribune* News Editor Parker Mize's comment: "I hope I shall never forget the stillness that settled over the newsroom at the death of Jim Russell. More than the absence of noise, it was the presence of quiet."

As for Bill Waymack, he early became a formidable character, his manner illustrating the way editors seemed to select promising staff members through a kind of trial by adversity. At the age of 21, a job-hunting 1926 graduate of the University of Iowa, Kenneth MacDonald, walked into the newsroom to see Waymack, then managing editor. "He was busy typing and didn't want to be disturbed," MacDonald said. "He was forbidding-looking, wearing a ragged old sweater and he hadn't shaved for a day or two. 'We don't have anything at all,' Waymack said, and resumed typing. I said: 'There must be something I can do. You must have vacation jobs, or something of the sort.' He replied irritably: 'No, there aren't.' Then he said: 'Rex Large [the news editor] is looking for an experienced copyreader. You don't think you could fill that job do you?' I said: 'I could try.' He said 'No, no,' and went back to his typing. I was just left standing there."

Not ready to give up, MacDonald left Waymack's office, saw News Editor Large in the newsroom and introduced himself, saying that Waymack had told him that Large was looking for a copyreader. When Large questioned him about his experience, MacDonald said he had worked on the student paper at the University of Iowa and had been graduated in journalism.

"That was almost a derogatory remark in those days," MacDonald said. "Oldtime newspapermen scorned journalism schools.... Large asked: 'Did they teach you that a newspaperman never makes any money?' I said: 'Well, I don't think we ever got very much into the economics of the profession.' He said: 'I'm going to give you a piece of advice you will thank me for later. If you go back out on the street where you came in, and walk east a couple of blocks, you will come to the home office of a big insurance company. Go in there and get a job, and in 20 years you will thank me.'

"I said, 'Hell, I don't want to work for an insurance company.' He said: 'All right, come to work at 6 o'clock Monday night.' I came to work at six Monday scared to death that Waymack would see me there and wonder what I was doing. Every time I saw Waymack for several weeks afterward, I got behind a pillar so he wouldn't see me."

After the first night, Large said he would try MacDonald out "for a week or two." Just over 50 years later, MacDonald retired, having served as editor for 23 years.

On the lighter side of journalism, the first daily columns of Harlan Miller appeared in *The Register* in 1921 under the heading "Paragraphophone." That effort preceded his "Over the Coffee" column, which was launched later in the 1920s and which carried Miller's byline in *The Register* to two generations of readers.

His earliest columns — he was a notable, wide-ranging reporter as well — were marked by a gossipy lightness and fluffiness; others demonstrated how old some stories are. For example, a half century ago, Miller wrote about a janitor testifying in a trial about how his wife entertained other men during his absence from home, whereupon an absent-minded man in the audience snapped his fingers and said: "Now I know where I left my umbrella!"

Miller undoubtedly began the column at the suggestion of young John Cowles, who believed that such daily features improved the papers' readability, and who similarly urged Sec Taylor to start a sports column.

Garner W. (Sec) Taylor, the newspapers' notable and longtime sports editor, arrived Oct. 3, 1914 accompanied by a nickname earned while working as secretary to baseball clubs. He also arrived with editors' expectations that he would gather news at the Statehouse as well as handle sports. Sec, however, said he would take the *Register* job only if he could spend full time on sports. The editors yielded and Sec teamed up with Jack North — originally Jake Norenbersky — who came to *The Tribune* in 1915. The two-man sports "staff" wrote all the local and Iowa sports stories and the headlines on national stories.

Between them they turned out 13 sports sections a week, each working six days one week and seven the next, with one day off every two weeks, commonplace practice in those days.

Writing about his aversion to columns, Sec said: "When I first came on *The Register,* I sometimes had a column called 'Shaking the Lemon Tree' but abandoned it. It was a column of short notes, alleged wisecracks and quips. I didn't like it and I guess the readers didn't either, because nothing was said when I abandoned it.

"When John Cowles came on the paper in 1920, he kept suggesting that I write a column. I always had the idea that a column was either good or bad — that if it wasn't good it didn't deserve a place in the newspaper. There weren't more than a dozen columns in the entire country worth the space devoted to them.

"So I kept finding excuses. Finally John became so urgent that I decided I had better write a column occasionally if I wanted to keep my job." And that was how Sec came to write "Sittin' In With the Athletes," a column that drew such wide reader interest that even Sec was impressed.

The integrity of Taylor and the sports department was praised in a 1929 study by the Carnegie Foundation for the Advancement of Teaching that was titled "The Press and College Athletics." The study singled out a letter sent by Taylor to college sports correspondents in about 1925 urging honest sports coverage.

The letter said in part:

"We want every correspondent to understand that we do not expect him to give away secrets or betray his team or coach. However, neither do we want false stories or reports. We do not want a story that Jim Blood will not be able to play next Saturday because of an injured ankle when the correspondent, the coach and the entire campus know he will play. Nor do we want a story that the attack will be built around Blood when everyone on the campus knows he has a broken collarbone and will not play.

"We are not concerned in winning or losing games for any team through the news columns. What we want is the news, while it is fresh and still news. Remember, the Register and Tribune [Company], and not your college or coach, pays your monthly correspondence checks. Help us make our sports pages during the week more than mere propaganda sheets for the college."

The Carnegie study also pointed out that the daily *Register* circulation advanced from 106,000 to 109,000 in 1927-1928 while *The Sunday Register* went from 161,800 to 169,250 in the same period. The study's authors commented, in careful understatement: "The increases tend to show that an enlightened sports policy has not been fatal to circulation."

Even closer to home, Taylor concentrated on upgrading not only sports coverage but sport itself. His insistence on sports honesty showed to its best advantage in the machinations surrounding a 1939 heavyweight prizefight that lined up a former Des Moines hotel bellboy, Johnny Paychek, in a rematch with a New Zealander named Maurice Strickland.

Suspecting a "fix" to make a winner of Paychek, who had lost his first match with Strickland, Taylor confronted the principals in a pre-fight meeting at the old Hotel Chamberlain in Des Moines.

Unless he got assurances from all concerned that the match was going to be on the level, Taylor said he was going to expose the whole thing as a phony. He apparently got the assurances, despite the existence of involved and peculiar pre-fight financial arrangments.

Post-fight stories indicated the squabble was over the insistence of Paychek's manager, Harold Steinman, that Paychek be paid $10,000 before the fight as some kind of guarantee.

Register sports coverage indicated that the 14,000 fight fans at League Park saw a good match in which Paychek defeated Strickland legitimately "in as vicious a battle as was ever fought between heavyweights." Not until the day following the fight did Taylor write directly about a possible fix attempt. The fight not only was on the level, he wrote, it was "a great battle as well." Discussing "ugly rumors," he wrote about the money argument and the $10,000 demand made by Steinman, Paychek's manager.

Taylor did not blame Promoter P. L. (Pinkie) George for the furor, but said Paychek was "finished" in Des Moines partly because of the "acts his manager perpetrated."

Years earlier, in 1930, Taylor and other sports writers suspected that a scheduled fight between Italian heavyweight Primo Carnera and Bearcat Wright in Omaha was fixed in Carnera's favor. In a pre-fight story, Taylor wrote that the contest was scheduled for "ten three-minute acts" and that there was "considerable conjecture about the fight, particularly since there has been so much of a suspicious nature emanat[ing] from all the Italian's scraps."

Taylor's comments should not have caused much reaction, but they angered someone enough so that the *Register* sports editor reportedly was threatened with harm if he appeared at the arena on fight night. He went anyway and saw Carnera score a knockout against Wright. The threats against Taylor came to nothing, and Midwest sports figures learned early that staying on the level was the best policy when Sec Taylor was around.

Taylor was around as sports editor and columnist for more than 50 years. When he died in Florida on Feb. 26, 1965, at age 78, Sec Taylor was still sports editor and still writing "Sittin' In With the Athletes."

Beginning in the earliest Cowles-Ingham years, emphasis at *The Register* concentrated on upgrading staff, coverage and circulation. Waymack, Taylor, Darling and others strove to find better-educated, better-trained employees and to continue improving their performance.

Among moves to bolster the staff immediately after World War I was the hiring of a tall, courtly, mustached Englishman to take pictures for the newspapers. George Yates — who became a great photographer with a flair for the dramatic — was a one-of-a-kind staff member, the kind about whom every oldtimer on the papers has at least one favorite anecdote.

Born in Lancashire, England, near Manchester, in 1890, Yates emigrated to Canada in 1912. In the course of his travels, he went to South Dakota, where in 1916 he enlisted in the National Guard and was called to service on the Mexican border. Eventually he was assigned to Camp Dodge, north of Des Moines, as an officer with the 88th Division. He became an American citizen, went overseas with the 88th and served in France with the American Expeditionary Force's division of criminal investigation. He returned to Des Moines in 1919 and became the one-man photographic staff for *The Register* and *The Tribune*.

As he grew in his job and as photography became steadily more important in the newspaper world, Yates's serious side stressed improvements in staff. He insisted that photographers are newsmen as well as photographers; he urged requiring photographers to have college training as well as good photographic technique. In public, his serious side was subordinated to a flamboyant image that captured his co-workers' (and the public's) imaginations.

He rarely missed a chance to solve a photographic

problem inventively. In 1921, at the heavily guarded national convention of the American Legion in Kansas City, Yates took what he knew were some good pictures for his papers — and then "fainted."

Because U.S. Gen. John (Black Jack) Pershing and French Marshal Ferdinand Foch, the great Allied war commanders, were guests at the meeting, security men insisted that no one in the hall be allowed to enter or leave the building while the two celebrities were present. The train that was to take Yates's photographs to Des Moines was scheduled to leave shortly and Yates had to get his film aboard somehow. (The days of transmission of photographs by electronic means were far off).

So Yates sank to the floor, claiming he was really quite ill. Red Cross aides carried him — and his photographic plates, stashed under his coat — out of the building. He got to the railroad station in time, the editors got the film, and the readers next day got a timely view of Pershing and Foch side by side.

Yates knew when to be nervy. There is no doubt that he often risked his neck to get pictures. "The first thing I saw when I got to the fire that destroyed the old Kirkwood Hotel," one colleague said, "was George, hanging off a fire escape," getting a photograph.

"Yates was a grandstander, but he did produce," said Frank Eyerly, who was managing editor in the 1950s and 1960s. "There was nothing he liked better than a challenge. He became so well known in Iowa that he never needed a ticket to get into a football game. I've seen him walk through the gate and out onto the field at the University of Iowa without any credentials. Everybody knew him. You would see old George striding along and people bowing to him. He made a swell appearance. He could have been elected U.S. senator if he had run."

During World War II, *Register* editors sent Yates to Washington, D. C., to get a series of photographs of Iowans prominent in the government's war effort. Again he came up against a tight security network. "George decided to test his ability to get into either the War Department or the Navy Department without an official pass," one editor said. "He succeeded. He used an Oddfellows lodge card or something of the sort that was the size of the official pass. He waved the card at a guard in the usual manner of Yates that he belonged wherever he was — just as if he owned the place — and he walked right in."

For big photo jobs, Yates adopted the habit of dressing the part — he wore a fireman's coat and hat when he covered major fires, he had a Sherlock Holmes deerstalker hat for police stories and, when the editor of *The Times* of London visited Des Moines, George wore a bowler hat and spats when he went to photograph the man. No doubt that day he was the compleat Englishman. All his life, Yates retained a touch of his British accent, but when he spoke to someone from his native land, the "touch" became three times as pronounced as otherwise.

Yates never failed to exploit the opportunity to put on a show during the annual Des Moines parades of *Register* and *Tribune* carriers from across the state. Watched by crowds of spectators, he would perch atop an 18-foot stepladder to get pictures of the carriers marching down Locust Street.

"George was one of the best photographers I ever knew. He never gave up on an assignment," the late *Tribune* reporter Cliff Millen once said, citing the time he and Yates went out to get a photograph and a story of a man who obviously did not want his picture taken.

"We get to the house and they slam the door in our faces," Millen said. "George says: 'Well, we'll just sit down on the porch here.' So we sit the rest of the day, and George says: 'I'll meet you here at 9 in the morning.' So at 9 next morning we go back and sit on the front porch again. Sure enough, at 9:30, the guy sticks his head out the door and says: 'You guys might as well come in.' And we got the picture."

Yates developed a brief but cordial friendship with Charles Lindbergh when the famous flier visited the Iowa State Fair in the late 1920s. A dozen years later, Lindbergh returned to Des Moines to speak at a controversial meeting opposing American involvement in World War II. But he refused to pose for pictures. Yates, ever the supersalesman, sent in word that the photographer who took Lindbergh's picture at the fair all those years ago was outside. Lindbergh remembered and welcomed Yates, who got a photograph no one else could get.

Yates loved airplanes and often flew to story assignments in an era in which air travel was in open-cockpit planes. He always wore a flier's soft leather helmet on such occasions — and even after the introduction of cabin planes made such headgear unnecessary, he continued wearing his flying hat.

He did so much flying so early that by 1924 he had completed the aerial photography of all 99 Iowa county-seat cities and towns. Those pictures were great circulation-builders for the papers.

One circulation-builder in which Yates was involved was not such a happy experience. In the mid-Twenties, three planes piloted by airmen called the "World Fliers" were to pass over Des Moines on a globe-circling trip that covered several months, counting lengthy stopovers, but nevertheless fascinated the world's newspaper readers. Going around the earth by air in the 1920s was a superevent.

The planes were scheduled to fly over Des Moines late in the morning and Billy Hale, then associate managing editor, wanted pictures of the planes over the city taken fast enough to meet a noon deadline so that he could get them in that afternoon's *Tribune*.

"I got a plane and pilot out on East Thirtieth Street," Yates said. "The editors of *The Capital* had the same idea. When I got to the field, Don Cook, the *Capital* photographer, was taking off. But his motor conked out and he had to land." Yates still was on the ground when the world fliers' planes, unexpectedly early, were sighted coming over the horizon. His pilot took off hurriedly but got up only to the low altitude of 1,700 feet while the other planes soared over the city at a much higher altitude.

"I took some pictures, but I might as well have taken them from the ground," Yates said. His negatives showed little other than a blank sky. To recover the situation, unbeknownst to anyone, Yates pulled out of the files a set of larger pictures of the same planes photographed flying over Seattle, Washington, earlier in the trip and used a re-photographing process to superimpose the pictures on his own work. *The Tribune* ran the picture five columns wide on Page One and readers were pleased.

Managing Editor Bill Waymack was *not* pleased. Relying on the sixth sense characteristic of the best newsmen, Waymack called Yates into his office and asked him if he had faked the picture. When Yates said he had, Waymack pointed out that while such practices might have been permitted in the newspaper business at one time, "we don't want that sort of thing on a responsible paper like *The Tribune*. Suppose *The Capital* should get wise to this? If *The Capital* does, you had better take your little black box and look elsewhere for greener pastures."

For several days, Yates and Waymack watched *The*

Capital for an expose, but their rivals didn't discover what Yates had done, and he was able to relax.

When *The Register* and *The Tribune* bought their own plane in 1928, Yates was as proud as anyone else around the newsroom. The five-place Fairchild, named the *Good News* in a reader contest, cruised at 75 miles per hour and had a top speed of 100 m.p.h., fast for its time.

Charles W. Gatschet, a test pilot for aircraft manufacturers, a U.S. air corps veteran of World War I and a former barnstormer with Lindbergh, joined the paper as a pilot who could take photographs and write stories as well. Charlie was safety-minded and a stickler for punctuality; he left at scheduled departure times to cover stories whether reporters or photographers had reached the airport or not.

Gatschet thought the purchase of the *Good News* was putting the cart before the horse; there were few airports in Iowa in 1928. He refused to land in pastures and avoided stunt flying, but in 1929 had a close call in a crash involving a plane-to-plane refueling test over Des Moines. One man was killed; Gatschet was thrown clear of one of the planes and parachuted to safety.

In the first *Good News*, Gatschet, Yates and reporter Bill Churchill flew to Kansas City in 1929 on what was, for the times, an adventurous assignment: Get pictures and a story on the *Graf Zeppelin,* the huge German dirigible, which was on a world tour. At the end of his more than 40 years with the papers, Yates was still calling this assignment the greatest thrill in his career.

When they arrived over Kansas City, the Iowans found 30 other planes in the murky sky, photographing the big lighter-than-air craft. The situation looked dicey to Gatschet so he flew out of the area and "hid" in a cloud. The dirigible's commander, who did not like the crowded sky any better, pulled up and out of altitude range of the small planes. When the light craft had all left, the *Graf Zeppelin* drifted down again to a lower level. At a strategic moment, the *Good News* flew out of the cloud cover and Yates shot numerous pictures even though someone on the dirigible waved a red flag at the Iowa plane. The *Graf Zeppelin* floated northeastward and Yates took photographs all the way to Ottumwa, Iowa.

In 14 years with the papers, Charlie Gatschet flew seven progressively more advanced *Good News* planes. He was the paper's pilot until the Dec. 7, 1941, Japanese attack on

Pearl Harbor, Hawaii, when he rejoined the air corps and was sent to the China-Burma-India war theater. He was killed at Karachi in April, 1945, in the crash of a C-46 cargo plane.

When George Yates died in 1968 at the age of 77, his obituary cited his development of the "machine-gun" photo technique as one of his major contributions to newspaper photography. In 1934, Managing Editor Stuffy Walters was impressed by the emotional impact of some still photographs made from newsreel film shot during the assassination in Marseilles of Yugoslavia's King Alexander I and French Foreign Minister Jean-Louis Barthou. The stills were fuzzy but effective nevertheless, so Walters asked Yates to try to develop a still camera with a shutter fast enough to get a series of action-sequence photographs that would be sharply focused.

Within a few weeks, Yates had built a superfast "machine gun" camera. It was put into use in the 1935 football season, giving sports-section readers sequences of pictures showing how key plays worked — or didn't work — in major football games. For newspaper readers, the photographs created the sense of participation that television's "instant replay" technique offers today. The sequence technique lent itself easily to diagramming, in which *The Register* and *The Tribune* pioneered. Under Yates's direction, *The Sunday Register* began to publish more football action pictures than any other newspaper in the country.

Action was the spur, too, for Stuffy Walters, another legendary character with the Cowles papers in their formative years. Walters joined *The Tribune* as news editor in 1928, advanced to managing editor and later went to Minneapolis after the Cowleses bought *The Minneapolis Star*. His idea of a fascinating story was the coverage he turned out for a 1934 "stratosphere" balloon flight from Rapid City, S. D. He turned loose reporters and photographers with abandon, despite the event's distance from Des Moines.

Opinions about Walters and his abilities and effectivness varied — as they do about and among most newspaper people. Frank Eyerly, who worked for Walters as telegraph editor before eventually becoming the papers' managing editor, regarded him as "an undereducated windmill," but was willing to salute his enthusiasm. Walter Graham, Sunday editor in the 1930s, thought Walters was great, as did Carl Gartner, who was a fine writer himself and an excellent picture editor.

Eyerly found Walters "a tremendous catalyst or sparkplug." He added: "He was a fellow who promoted action. I find it very difficult to discount him and say he was no good because that isn't true.

"He had powers of enthusiasm plus a sparkplug personality, but he was completely lacking in depth and understanding of serious problems. He really did not know much about people."

In an interview late in life after his own retirement, Stuffy Walters said: "I was very conscious of the fact that I was not Frank's favorite, but that didn't make any difference to me. I thought Frank was a fine newspaperman. I had the feeling that Frank was too highbrow for my type of journalism. I was a cornball."

Billy Hale, the same breed of action journalist as Walters, frequently made life miserable for editors and reporters on both papers. Gardner Cowles in 1917 had hired Hale away from the rival *Des Moines News,* where he had been a columnist as well as editor. Cowles put Hale in charge of the *Tribune* operation.

"There never was a dull day with Billy," said reporter and later City Editor Rodney Selby. "He had the ability to lift the appealing or the strange in the actions of men and women out of even the most prosaic news. It may not have been great journalism, but it was warm and it suited Des Moines."

Hale could not stand dullness. Even "quiet" stories were written with briskness — but fortunately not usually in the fashion of the suicide story that bore the souped-up headline: "Booze-Crazed Fireman Dies With Neck in Noose."

When he was a young reporter fresh out of college, the youngest of the Cowles brothers, Mike, experienced Hale's enterprise more than once. "In the first assignment he ever gave me," Mike Cowles said, "Billy told me to go find a boy who had been totally blind since birth and take him to the Ringling Brothers circus. I was told to write the boy's reaction to the circus. I didn't get much of a story. The little blind boy was more interested in the gear shift of my car than in touching the elephant's trunk."

Another story idea involved a suspect in a murder case. "The guy was in jail at Boone," Mike Cowles said. "Hale talked the sheriff into putting me in jail with the fellow.

Billy said: 'You stay there a couple of hours and then write up your impressions.' " The prisoner was not impressed. "He said he was going to beat me up," Mike Cowles said. "The sheriff had left for a couple of hours. There was nobody around the jail. The guy scared hell out of me. I was really glad to get out of there."

Hale was not often bested in the fierce Des Moines newspaper circulation battles of the era — his *Tribunes* were exciting, violent, human. They were well illustrated with photographs and the stories were written in short, simple sentences that made easy reading.

Hale was interested chiefly in local and Iowa news, attempting to get twice as many local names into his paper as either *The Capital* or *The News,* and usually succeeding.

The senior Gardner Cowles regarded Hale as a genius within narrow limits and a strong force for building circulation under Managing Editor Waymack. Another company executive described Hale's talents succinctly: "Billy did not know a damn thing about national affairs and cared less. But he knew the East Side and South Des Moines and North High School. He got around town and he knew everybody."

He knew his staff, too, and often posted stories containing errors — wrong names, wrong spellings — on a bulletin board to keep reporters up to the mark. He did not spare Mike Cowles, whose mistakes went up on the board, too.

"You had to have extrasensory perception in those days to survive as a reporter," said *Tribune* reporter Bill Millhaem. "If you got scooped more than once, Billy fired you. Billy fired them faster than Waymack could hire them."

Despite assorted differences, Millhaem admired Hale. So did Cliff Millen, who joined the *Tribune* staff in 1923 and almost immediately found himself in a tough ads-vs.-news situation. A big advertiser who was being tried in Municipal Court on a charge of assaulting a waitress in a downtown cafe was threatening to get Millen fired if he reported the story. Millen phoned in the facts and the story ran.

"After work that day," Millen said, "I went in and sat by Billy Hale's desk waiting to get fired. Nothing happened then or the next day. The third day I asked Billy if the advertiser had been in. Hale said yes, the fellow had been in, but he sent him on his way without giving him any satisfaction."

Millen, who had planned to stay in Des Moines for a two-year stint, was "impressed to find a paper so independent of pressure" in those times. He worked for *The Tribune* the rest of his newspaper life.

Billy Hale showed his violent side — with good cause — on the day that a call came in at noon that an elevator in Des Moines' Randolph Hotel had fallen and four persons had been killed. Although Hale had established a rule that all *Tribune* reporters were not permitted to go to lunch at the same time, there wasn't a reporter in the newsroom. All of them had gone across Locust Street to lunch at the Boekenhoff Cafe.

Hale lost his temper, picked up the nearest hefty object and hurled it through a newsroom window. The sound of shattering glass penetrated to the cafe, the reporters came running, Hale organized the coverage, and *The Tribune* that evening carried a complete story on the disaster.

Other legendary exploits centered on the *Register* newsroom. They were amusing, free-lance, strictly unofficial — and frowned-up on if discovered officially. They smack of some of the quieter exploits of "The Front Page" and, like that play and its characters, would be frivolous and detrimental to today's more serious tone.

John Grimes was a zany copyreader who habitually cast about for ways to relieve the monotony of his editing task — shortening stories and writing headlines. He began his quixotic career as a jokester by founding the Society for the Prevention of Cruelty to Belgian Hares after he had edited a story about a Chicago neighborhood that planned an extermination campaign against the multitudinous progeny of a pair of Belgian hares.

Grimes later had his hands full trying to stay out of trouble over Count Giavanno Reichivicci, his masterpiece creation.

Grimes was working on copy on a *Register* afternoon shift when he came across a story about an Italian wrestler named Giavanno Reichivicci, who was coming to the United States. The name fascinated Grimes, and, as he was musing over its rhythms, he was assigned to edit a society page story that included a list of guests at a social function. Without telling anyone — and strictly against the rules — he added "Count Giavanno Reichivicci" to the guest list.

After the paper had been printed, Grimes showed the story to a fellow worker and said, testing: "Remember that Italian wrestler? A funny thing happened. He attended a party in Des Moines." No one reported the incident, and Grimes became obsessed with getting the name into the newspaper. "The name appeared in lists of guests at weddings," a Grimes contemporary recalled. "The Count was also listed among those attending a house party at Lake Okoboji," the popular Iowa resort area.

The Count acquired a distinctive personality and style. In some *Register* stories he was described as a "world-famous collector of jade" and the holder of "The Order of Procurers of the Sacred Stone." Had his whimsy been detected by the top editors, Grimes would have been in deep trouble. But no one ever protested to the editors that a guest list was wrong, that no Count had attended his party.

"Looking into it afterward, we came to the conclusion that hostesses were proud to have had a Count listed among their guests," one veteran editor said. "They never let on to anyone that he hadn't been present. Some people actually were under the impression that they had met and talked with the Count. They said he was a fine fellow in every respect."

The restless, unpredictable Grimes got fed up with his copy-editing job late one afternoon in 1934, on a payday. He got his check at 5:45 and told the editors he was going to a drugstore a half-block away to cash the check. He walked out the door and was never seen again at *The Register*.

Des Moines newsmen knew that he was working somewhere, because Count Giavanno Reichivicci appeared periodically in stories that came to the notice of *Register* staff members. As far as Des Moines newsmen could determine, the final story had to do with the discovery of a tree in the Amazon jungle "from which flowed pure kerosene." Discoverer of the tree was, of course, Count Reichivicci, "the world-famous collector of jade and authority on plant life in the Amazon Valley." Tragedy marred the Count's discovery, the story said; his guide struck a match in the bush to enable the Count to examine the tree more closely and the kerosene exploded, killing the guide and burning off the Count's eyebrows. As soon as Reichivicci recovered from his burns, the story added, he planned to return to the United States to prepare another expedition into the jungle to find more kerosene trees.

The Count's name never appeared in print again — but a rumor in the newspaper world said a Count Reichivicci might have been among the unidentified dead in a railroad wreck in an eastern state.

11 THE FINEST DECADE

Gardner Cowles, sr., and Harvey Ingham moved into their seventies in the 1930s, gradually giving way to the younger generation. Ingham approached the change with characteristic good humor. "I am making up my mind not to become a disgruntled old man," he said.

As early as 1928, Ingham had begun clearing the decks, selling his common stock in the Register and Tribune Company to Gardner Cowles. In 1932, the elder Cowles, eager "to see this large indebtedness against the Register and Tribune paid off while I am still here and able to attend to business," asked Ingham to exchange his substantial holdings in Register and Tribune Company bonds for U.S. government securities and Iowa road bonds owned by the company.

In the newsroom, by 1930 Ingham had relinquished many of his duties as editor although he carried the title until 1943, when he was named editor emeritus and Bill Waymack was appointed editor. Ingham turned direction of the editorial pages over to Waymack in 1930 and for the next dozen years wrote a signed column for *The Register*'s editorial page.

Ingham stepped down partly on the advice of his doctor, who said the 72-year-old editor was no longer able to follow his previous arduous routine. For several years, Ingham and Waymack had been writing all the editorials and editing the editorial pages of both papers and also handling the time-consuming task of editing letters to the editor.

Ingham's column reflected the Depression times and temper. In 1930, Ingham wrote: "Where hunger rages, there is never going to be established order no matter what the form of government." In 1931, he was in the vanguard as usual, confronting the problem of joblessness. He asked a question that millions of unemployed Americans were asking in less measured tones: "If private enterprise fails us at any time of stagnation, must not the community step in and afford employment?" Few citizens in those days believed that government had any business providing jobs for the unemployed.

He did not fret about growing centralization of power in 1932, when he wrote: "In the large, it can not be said that expanding national control has really lessened the rights of the individual or deprived the local community of its proper control."

Forward-looking as ever, even at 79, he urged meeting new challenges. In 1937, he wrote: "It pays to try new things once in a while, merely because they are new. They arouse public interest and render service in that way if no other." In 1938, as the Nazi totalitarian menace grew internationally and as economic problems remained formidable nationally, he took the contemplative view: "In times like these, when nobody can look to the immediate future with confidence, what is better worthwhile than to take the long view and, realizing what man has done in his 7,000 years of recorded history ... speculate a little on what the next 7,000 years may mean. And at that, 7,000 years are purely incidental. Man has a long future ahead of him, and apparently he is gaining more and more control over his own destiny."

A tribute in 1934 given by the Drake University chapter of Phi Beta Kappa, which made him an honorary member, focused on his career and his philosophy. Summarizing his life and his thought, the citation honoring him listed "three notable phases of public discussion" in Ingham's editorial writing.

The first: "No one ... has had a more lively appreciation and intimate knowledge of the history of the wrongs of the aboriginal races resident among us, and voiced such just criticism of the gross wrongs inflicted upon the Indians. ..."

The second: "In the treatment of the perplexities arising out of the abolishment of slavery in this country, no editor ... has been more straightforward and staunch in demanding just consideration for the Negro in his life among us."

And third: "In the vexations and harassing problems of international peace and the proper course for us of these United States to pursue, you have invariably stood for broad humanitarian policies, for fair dealing and peaceful procedure in settling international disputes."

From within the Register and Tribune Company family other tributes came. In 1937, Gardner Cowles wrote to Ingham: "My long association with you has been one of the finest things of my life." And in 1944, Mrs. Cowles wrote: "It was a lucky day for the Cowles family, as well as for the Inghams when you moved to Des Moines. It was also a lucky day for Iowa when you began directing the thought of the people into right and wholesome channels."

While columnist Ingham was philosophizing and his fellow editorialists were taking the long view, the news side of *The Register* was covering the 1930s' unusually large ration of depression, disillusion and disaster and influencing the way Iowans saw the world and dealt with it.

The 1930s were the last and finest decade of the era of Gardner Cowles and Harvey Ingham. The policies they had planted to nurture the professional purpose of a newspaper — to supply the reader with complete, understandable and clearly written news — came to fruition during a period that called for close coverage of important events. The 1930s were exciting, frustrating, frightening, complex; readers were angry, despondent, puzzled, and eager for authoritative news on issues that affected them directly.

Low farm income brought the state to the brink of revolution, banks closed by the hundreds, high tax rates were beyond available income, massive unemployment burdened cities and towns, mortgage foreclosures took homes from thousands of citizens.

From 1933 onward, Democratic President Franklin Roosevelt's New Deal launched far-reaching projects — federal farm programs, rural electrification, public welfare programs, public power projects, bank-deposit insurance, stock-market regulation, mortgage-foreclosure protection. On some issues, newspaper reports were so eagerly awaited out in the state that banks posted pages of *The Register* or *The Tribune* in their windows to keep townspeople up to date. In some areas, the demand for papers occasionally proved greater than the supply.

Richard Wilson of *The Register*'s Washington Bureau and *Register* Farm Editor J S. Russell did what probably was the best reporting in the United States on the new federal agricultural programs established by President Roosevelt and his agriculture secretary, Iowan Henry A. Wallace. Besides being able to deal with Wallace, Wilson had another close contact in the Agriculture Department in a Wallace assistant, James Le Cron — a former Register and Tribune Company official and a Cowles son-in-law.

The decade was ideal for news but difficult financially. All over the country in 1933, advertising slumped to a level 45 per cent below 1929's. Register and Tribune Company profits dropped near the vanishing point, Mike Cowles told a company group years later.

Paradoxically, more and more Iowans subscribed to the newspapers, the result of the work of good news staffs, the eagerness for news and features — among the least expensive entertainments available — and of hard-driving circulation efforts.

In March of 1929, at the height of pre-Crash prosperity, *The Sunday Register*'s circulation averaged 185,775. By March of 1932, a year of disaster in many other lines of work, the Sunday paper's weekly circulation soared to 218,200, up more than 32,000 copies, or 17 per cent, in three years. During the next year, the Sunday paper lost 8,000 circulation, but by March of 1934, it had rebounded with a gain of nearly 40,000 copies.

Much of that resurgence was easy to explain. The New Deal's shift in the country's focus of power to Washington stimulated Iowans' appetites for news of programs that concerned the improvement of their daily lives. As News Editor Stuffy Walters put it: "Iowa no longer was being run out of the Statehouse but out of Washington." Mike and John Cowles realized, well before many other Midwestern editors, the necessity of installing their own full-time man in Washington to report and interpret fast-breaking news in terms of how it affected Iowans; the wire services and special correspondent's stories were not enough.

Mike Cowles chose 28-year-old Richard Wilson, *The Register*'s city editor, to open a *Register* and *Tribune* news bureau in Washington in September, 1933. The move was in recognition, said an editorial, of "the tremendous importance of Washington news to the people of Iowa in this extraordinary period."

It was typical of the Cowleses to take on the added costs of maintaining the bureau in a year when the papers barely broke even. They regarded the action as a news obligation. In the editorial announcing establishment of the bureau, the publishers said: "Nobody knows how far [the] concentration of economic and political management of the country is going to go. But everybody knows that the great experiment will last for a long time in one form or another. It is the obligation of these papers to the state to give such news service from every quarter as they have never given before, and that applies with particular force to Washington news with an Iowa slant."

Richard Wilson's first major Washington story was carried under an eight-column banner: "Wallace For Limited Inflation." Agriculture Secretary Henry A. Wallace, Wilson reported, believed in using inflationary procedures to boost prices of farm products and other items from the Depression's disastrously low levels. Wallace warned, however, that inflation by itself was no cure-all for the nation's ills in 1933.

Wilson stories appeared on Page One of *The Register* three times in the next seven days. They ranged in subject matter from the Federal Deposit Insurance Corp. to Reconstruction Finance Corporation bank aid to an exclusive Wilson story on the possibility of federal farm-price supports.

Wilson and other bureau reporters over the years did not try to cover the complete Washington scene; there was no point in duplicating Washington stories received in Des Moines from the Associated Press and other wire services. Instead, *Register* bureau staff members always have tried — with considerable success — to produce "exclusive in-depth stories" of interest to Iowans. Wilson and his subsequent staff frequently beat the wire services and everyone else on major national stories.

Wilson was first with details on the New Deal's proposed farm program — a matter of great interest to Midwestern farmers — and he forecast the defeat of F.D.R.'s Supreme Court-packing plan when U.S. Senator Clyde L. Herring of Iowa was a key figure in Roosevelt's controversy with Congress over the plan. An exclusive interview with presidential aide Harry Hopkins gave Wilson the first national break in 1938 on Roosevelt's unsuccessful effort to purge congressional leaders — including U.S. Senator Guy Gillette of Iowa — who had opposed the court-packing plan.

Early in his bureau career, which ended in 1975, Wilson set two goals for himself: To build up his contacts by seeing at least two news sources each day and to write two stories daily, one with an Iowa angle and a second of national scope.

His perseverance did not go without notice. Sometime during Wilson's first year or two in Washington, President

Roosevelt told a *Register* top executive: "Dick Wilson is one of the four best reporters in Washington." Dismissing the compliment as "standard Washington persiflage," Wilson said later that Roosevelt "barely knew who I was at the time."

Nevertheless, Wilson was one of the capital's top newsmen almost from the start. His awarding-winning coverage (he won a Pulitzer Prize in 1954 for a series of stories on Soviet espionage in the United States) was part and parcel of the *Register*'s broad view of the world.

Despite the heavy focus on interpretive news and exclusive stories from Washington as the 1930s advanced, there was plenty of other news during the decade to attract the Iowa reader interested in more than his own community.

One of the spectacular disaster stories of the decade was the fire June 27, 1931 that swept through the northern Iowa city of Spencer, touched off by an 11-year-old boy who dropped a lighted Fourth of July sparkler into a pile of fireworks in a drugstore.

Before it was dynamited to a halt, the fire destroyed 25 buildings and damaged 50 others in a four-and-a-half-block area. The last telegram sent from Spencer that afternoon before flames ate up the city's telegraph and telephone lines was a wire to *The Register,* whose airplane coverage was by that time a byword in Iowa.

"Town is burning," the telegram said. "Send plane with dynamite and fire chief. Water pressure is gone."

The fact that Spencer leaders instinctively turned for help to *The Register,* more than 150 miles away, demonstrated the growing acceptance across the state of the Des Moines newspapers. The Register and Tribune organization had become a well-known resource to which Iowans could turn in time of trouble.

Register editors received the telegraphed plea for aid at 5:02 p.m. Twenty-eight minutes later, the *Register* plane *Good News II* took off for Spencer, with Pilot Charlie Gatschet at the controls. Also aboard were photographer George Yates, reporters and the Des Moines fire chief. Two other planes left at the same time carrying explosives experts and other firefighters. Because federal aviation rules forbade it, none of the planes carried dynamite. At the request of *Register* editors, dynamite was rushed by truck from Primghar and Mason City, and firefighters used it to blow up buildings in the path of the fire and halt the flames.

The Register got part of its original story from Mike Cowles, who was vacationing at Lake Okoboji, some 18 miles north of Spencer. The *Good News* reporter-photographer team spent 45 minutes at the scene, flew back to Des Moines and got their story and photographs into the next day's *Sunday Register.* Covering that kind of story in those days in a total of four hours' flying and coverage time was quite a feat, and the editors capitalized on it by spreading the story all over the Sunday paper.

In 1936, fires on July 4 devastated Oyens and Remsen, neighboring towns in northwest Iowa. Remsen town officials appealed frantically to *The Sunday Register* for help, and again dynamite was trucked in to stop the fires. In 1937, the Iowa Legislature outlawed all fireworks in the state except those used in supervised displays.

The 1930s were an era of airplane expansion for the papers. Register and Tribune Company planes that flew the Iowa skies during that era included a strange craft, an autogiro. It was soon dubbed the "Flying Windmill" because it was kept aloft by a whirling overhead four-blade rotor, somewhat similar to that of the modern helicopter. Christened *Good News III,* it drew large crowds at the Iowa State Fair and at airports all over the state.

The crash of another breed of flying craft, the giant dirigible *Hindenburg,* nearly as long as three football fields, provided the occasion for one of the most visually impressive editions published in Des Moines. On May 7, 1937, *The Register* contained a series of Wirephotos of the crash that showed the effectiveness of photojournalism. Page One consisted almost entirely of one big picture, the full eight-column width, showing a huge blast of fire flashing upward as the lighter-than-air craft burst into flames and crashed while landing at Lakehurst, N. J. On that May 6, it was completing its first transatlantic crossing from Europe of the 1937 season. Of the passengers and crew members aboard, 36 eventually were counted among the dead; 61 survived, most of them by jumping while the fiery skeleton of the ship was still 15 or 20 feet off the ground.

Inside that *Register* were many of the striking pictures that came over the wires. Realizing that the photographs they were receiving would bring the disaster home to readers with great immediacy (in the manner of, but with more permanence than, today's television coverage) *Register* editors used great quantities of visual art. All told, that *Register* contained 26 illustrations and photographs — from the newly developed Associated Press Wirephoto setup and from *New York Times* sources.

Mike Cowles, then executive editor of the papers, and his wife had returned from Germany on the *Hindenburg* almost exactly a year before, and his story of the dirigible's fine flight characteristics but terrible fire danger brought Iowa readers a close-up view of an actual flight on the doomed craft.

Spectacular though they were, conflagrations, crashes and crimes like the Thirties' many bank robberies did not dominate the conscious life of the decade.

Far more important to Americans and Iowans was the economic sickness of the nation and the world, which spawned revolts among the normally law-abiding Iowa citizenry. Agriculture had suffered through 10 years of low prices and deflation and tens of thousands of farmers had lost their land through mortgage foreclosures. In the five-year period between Mar. 15, 1926, and Mar. 15, 1931, one Iowa farmer in seven lost his farm though foreclosure, *Register* Farm Editor J S. Russell reported. "These foreclosures affected 33,000 farms and a total of more than five million acres," he wrote, quoting a report based on a U.S. Agriculture Department survey. At the same time, interest rates advanced from 5 per cent to 5½ per cent on farm loans. The situation was so hopeless for some farmers, Russell wrote, that they insisted that the mortgage holder take over the land without going through legal proceedings.

Farmers were driven to fighting back against forces they could not control. Iowa's celebrated 1931 "Cow War" was the state's first major rural violence of the 1930s. State veterinary officials had launched a state-wide testing campaign to locate and eliminate all tuberculous cattle, an obvious threat to human beings. Fearing for their herds, some farmers insisted that the tests were unreliable. Some 1,200 farmers traveled to Des Moines to try to persuade the Legislature to make the state law on bovine-tuberculosis testing optional with the farmer. The Legislature refused, in the face of a long protest at the Statehouse.

Several months later, Cedar County farmers attacked veterinarians at work and halted testing. Gov. Dan Turner called out the National Guard, declared martial law in Cedar County, and the veterinarians completed testing in Cedar and other counties under the protection of National Guardsmen.

The Register meanwhile was counseling reason. "Iowans throughout the state will regret the resort to martial law," the paper said editorially. "Yet no other course was open to the governor.... The law requiring the testing of cattle for tuberculosis resulted not from despotism but from democratic procedures. It was intended not to oppress farmers but to protect the milk consumers of the state, including the farmers and their families."

The farmer was regarded in some quarters as "the forgotten man." President Herbert Hoover, who got strong editorial support from *The Register,* came in for heavy criticism, along with his party, at the 1932 national Republican convention in Chicago for paying too much attention to the still-live question of Prohibition of liquor while agriculture faced a ruinous future. As production costs outstripped the actual prices farmers were getting for their commodities, some militant farmers joined the new "Farmers Holiday Association" and went "on strike," blockading highways in efforts to prevent commodities from reaching markets, thereby holding down supplies and, it was hoped, raising prices. Bruising confrontations developed as lawmen broke up highway protests and arrested some of the "pickets." Anger rose as farmers who did not want to join the "strike" protested the pickets' actions.

The protests and clashes gained recognition for the farmer and both 1932 presidential candidates, incumbent President Herbert Hoover, the West Branch, Iowa, native, and Democrat Franklin D. Roosevelt came to Iowa to try to rally farmers to their causes. Hoover, in a speech in the old Des Moines Coliseum, promised to try to find a way to refinance farm mortgages as a check against foreclosures. Roosevelt spoke at Sioux City, a good choice because the packinghouse city had been under virtual siege for a 30-day period by "Farmers Holiday" protesters and was the focus of farmer dissatisfaction with President Hoover.

The 1932 Hoover-Roosevelt campaign was a good test of the *Register*'s effort to separate its opinion from its news columns. Though the corporate heart was editorially with Hoover, *The Register* and *The Tribune* devoted considerable space to Roosevelt's speech at Sioux City Sept. 29, 1932, in which he advocated lower tariff rates that he said were helping swell industrial profits at the expense of farmers. He also proposed tax reductions and improved government efficiency, but, *The Register* said editorially, he failed to clarify his farm relief plan. Both papers gave extensive picture coverage to the Roosevelt sortie into the farm belt as well.

Hoover — he was, after all, both a native son and the incumbent president — got a bigger welcome both publicly and in the press with his Coliseum appearance and the papers stood by him editorially through the campaign.

Meanwhile, Gardner Cowles, by now a member of the federal Reconstruction Finance Corporation board, tried to help bolster the Hoover cause with an R.F.C. announcement declaring that efforts were being made to fill the Iowa need for a new agency to make loans on farm land to Iowans.

And, though his newspapering principles required separation of news and editorial content, Gardner Cowles did not abdicate his right as a private citizen — a powerful one — to support his choice.

Cowles was so worried about the chances for success of the Hoover visit to Des Moines, scheduled for Oct. 4, 1932, that he telephoned his youngest son in Des Moines and said: "Mike, in spite of the fact that the farmers are in rebellion, President Hoover has decided he wants to come to . . . Iowa and make a major farm speech. You are going to organize things. I want you to see to it personally that the Coliseum is full that night."

In the light of Hoover's unpopularity, the assignment to fill the 9,500-seat Coliseum was a tough one. Mike Cowles and Iowa American Legion officials Hanford MacNider and Frank Miles recruited 1,000 to 2,000 Iowa Legionnaires, brought them by bus to Des Moines, gave them free dinners and put them in the first 10 rows at the Coliseum. "We wanted to give an impression of great enthusiasm," Mike Cowles said. "We told them how to cheer."

Cowles also called Republican chairmen of 50 central Iowa counties and asked each to charter a bus and bring 60 to 70 "good Republicans" to Des Moines. "If they were unable to raise the money locally, I would get a committee to raise the cash," he said. "I wanted them here and I wanted each bus full. That worked pretty well, too."

Next, Cowles called Iowa Republican Gov. Dan Turner, who, Cowles knew, was privately bitter about Hoover. Turner wanted no part of Hoover but did agree to talk further with Cowles at the governor's residence. "Fortunately, Mrs. Turner sided with me," Cowles recalled later. "The governor finally agreed that he and Mrs. Turner would give a dinner party for the Hoovers before the

Coliseum meeting, but he refused to invite anyone else but me." Five persons, the Hoovers, the Turners and Mike Cowles, sat down that evening at what may have been the chilliest dinner party in the history of Des Moines.

"My God, five people! . . . It was cold as hell," Cowles said. "Hoover didn't say anything and Turner didn't say anything. Mrs. Hoover, Mrs. Turner and I did all the talking. [But] I couldn't get Turner to introduce Hoover that evening at the Coliseum."

The meal ended so quickly that the Secret Service got the Hoovers, the Turners and Cowles to the Coliseum too early and the Hoovers and Cowles were taken to a room back of the stage.

"Hoover at that point knew he was getting the hell whipped out of him in the presidential race," Cowles said. "He had absolutely no stomach for making a speech that night. He sat waiting with his head in his hands, all dejected and depressed. Mrs. Hoover walked over, took him by the shoulders and shook him. She snapped: 'Herbert! Straighten up and be a man!' She had a lot of steel in her. He straightened up and started pacing the floor."

Hoover delivered an excellent speech to a nearly full house that night and nationwide radio listeners heard enthusiastic applause and no jeers from the audience that Mike Cowles helped build.

The Register the next morning devoted nearly the whole of Page One to Hoover headlines, stories and pictures, kicked off with coverage of a big downtown parade in the afternoon that had drawn 120,000 spectators. It also covered, on a "second-day" basis, an anti-Hoover story to which the afternoon *Tribune* had given full coverage the afternoon before. The subject was a rival "Farmers Holiday" parade that rolled through downtown Des Moines earlier on Oct. 4. Several thousand protesters joined in the parade, which included a procession of 100 or so automobiles and 59 trucks bearing signs like:

"In Hoover We Trusted; Now We Are Busted"

"Clinton County — 1,700 Insolvent Farmers"

No matter how enthusiastic the welcome, Hoover's career in elective office was ending. The market pages the day he was in Des Moines showed why, in part. The top price paid for hogs in Des Moines on Oct. 4, 1932 was a wretchedly low $3.50 per 100 pounds. In Chicago, the price was only $3.75. Cattle ranged from $6 to $8.25 a hundredweight. No. 2 corn brought only 19½ to 20 cents a bushel in

Des Moines, 15½ to 16 at country elevators.

Perhaps the best insight into the situation was expressed that day by Mark Sullivan in his syndicated Washington column on *The Register* editorial page. In an analysis that must have chilled Republican hearts but which followed the paper's policy of candid journalism, he wrote: "The political color of the West is determined by the mood of the farmer. The mood of the farmer is determined by the Depression.... As of this date, the amount of discontent is formidable.... The roughly half of the farmers who have mortgages on their farms are in deep and acute distress. They can not pay interest or principal with the prices of crops where they now are.... Foreclosure is the result and foreclosure gives rise in the farmers to that peculiarly acute resentment which is accompanied by a justified sense of wrong."

Sullivan declared — as Hoover had in his Des Moines speech — that some of the joint stock land banks were being heartless about foreclosures. The columnist told of a recent Jay Darling cartoon portraying a land bank as "a turkey buzzard with a protruding stomach, sitting on a limb watching a foreclosure proceeding and remarking with well-fed satisfaction: 'It's a good depression.' "

That cartoon, Sullivan wrote, reflected the views of "so well-balanced and thoughtfully edited" a paper as *The Des Moines Register*.

Just as the paper did not hesitate to publish the column and the cartoon, it did not shortchange former U.S. Senator James A. Reed of Missouri, who came to Des Moines the following week to answer Hoover. A Page One banner headline summed up Reed's attack at a Coliseum meeting of 5,000 Democrats: "Hoover False Prophet, Says Reed."

Register writer C. C. Clifton predicted, despite a poll to the contrary, that Hoover would win Iowa's 11 electoral votes. For one of the few times in what eventually was a 38-year career as a *Register* political writer, Clifton missed. Roosevelt won 598,000 Iowa votes to Hoover's 414,000, and swept Democrats into most state offices. The Democrats captured the U.S. Senate seat, the governorship, all of the other elective state offices, state Supreme Court judgeships and six of the nine Iowa congressional seats. In the Legislature and the county courthouses, Democrats scored impressive gains, too. Never had the Republicans taken such a beating in Iowa.

Editorially, *The Register* said it "accepts the verdict so

decisively given and wishes Governor Roosevelt a most successful administration."

The farm violence continued into 1933. On Jan. 4, more than 300 farmers converged on a farm mortgage sale in the Plymouth County courthouse in Le Mars, in northwestern Iowa. Le Mars attorney Herbert Martin submitted a $30,000 bid for a farm property, $3,000 less than the farmer's mortgage obligation. The additional debt was called a "deficiency judgment." When the bid was announced, *The Register* reported, the farmers "fell upon attorney Martin and dragged him from the courthouse steps. . . . A rope was swung before him and lynching was suggested unless he raised his bid to the face of the mortgage and the costs."

By telegraph, Martin got the life insurance company he was representing in the mortgage case to agree to raising the bid. But the farmers were not finished. Scores went to the courtroom where District Judge C. W. Pitts was sitting and "demanded that he refuse to sign foreclosure or deficiency judgment decrees, accompanying their demands with threats." The judge offered to recommend to Iowa Governor-elect Clyde L. Herring that the law be changed to delay mortgage foreclosures. The farmers accepted that and left.

The Jan. 4 triumph at Le Mars heartened the farm protesters in that area and set the stage for later and more spectacular acts of violence.

While expressing understanding of the plight of the farmers, *The Register* disapproved of the use of force.

"Exercise of physical duress against an agent who is merely performing his duty is not to be condoned," an editorial said. "And certainly nobody who believes in law and order can excuse even the suggestion of a threat against a judge who is conscientiously enforcing the law as it is written. Yet even Judge Pitts and the Plymouth County Bar have gone out of their way to manifest their sympathy with the purposes of the Le Mars farmers."

The Register pointed out that corn prices were so low the entire 1932 Iowa crop would bring only enough to pay "a fraction of a single year's interest" on the total mortgage debt in the state. "What further commentary is needed," the paper asked, "to understand the feeling of the Le Mars farmers who resorted the other day to methods that can not possibly be defended in behalf of a cause for which sympathy is universal?"

(Cash corn was worth only about 25 cents a bushel in Chicago in January, 1933, and about 15 cents a bushel in Iowa. Hog prices hovered around $3.40 per 100 pounds in Chicago and cattle around $5, with a top of nearly $7 per hundredweight.)

Governor Herring late in January issued a proclamation calling on all mortgage-holders and other creditors to refrain from foreclosures until the Legislature, then in session, had time to act. The proclamation was good psychology and did slow the foreclosure trend, but did not have legal standing. A friendly *Tribune* editorial called it "a formal appeal to make uniform the policy of intelligent leniency toward farm and other mortgage-givers that many mortgage holders have been exhibiting in recent months." The editorial added: "We are in a serious situation, threatening to drive many from their homes, all because of the great deflation for which our people are in no wise to blame."

On Mar. 13, 1933, more than 3,000 angry farmers poured into the halls of the Iowa Statehouse. The farmers charged that the lawmakers had been too slow in enacting farm-relief measures. Years later, State Representative Dewey Goode, a veteran Bloomfield Republican, told a reporter: "You didn't know what was going to happen that day. They were actually carrying pitchforks and ropes in some instances. But I don't think they had any intention of using them." (Ultimately, the 1933 Legislature did pass four laws to aid debt-ridden farmers, one of them permitting foreclosures to be delayed.)

On Apr. 27, 1933, the violence escalated. At Le Mars, a crowd of 100 farmers dragged Judge C. C. Bradley from his bench, took him out on a country road and threatened to hang him. He was beaten, smeared with axle grease and suffered rope burns from a noose that was tightened around his neck, but he "refused repeatedly to promise to sign no more mortgage foreclosure actions against farmers." Suddenly, the farmers appeared to realize what they had done. They scattered, leaving the judge to be picked up by a passing motorist, who took him back to Le Mars.

Earlier the same day, at Primghar, 44 miles northeast of Le Mars, many of the same farmers battled with 22 O'Brien County sheriff's deputies when the deputies barred the way to a forced farm sale in the courthouse.

The Register editorially called the incidents "an outrage against the great multitude of law-abiding farmers." The editorial continued *The Register*'s policy of urging concern for individual rights while insisting that protests be made within the system. It observed that the state was "acutely sympathetic" with the plight of the farmer and was backing "every legitimate demand of its farm population for relief. . . . But sympathy with the farm cause, which is the cause of all Iowa, is one thing and toleration of violent insurrection is a wholly different matter."

In the fall of 1933, despite the developing New Deal and the coming of welcome federal farm programs, farm pickets once again blocked highways and burned railway bridges in northwest Iowa. This time the protests ran into open and angry opposition from other farmers. *The Tribune* reported in November that 250 members of the farm-oriented "Mills County Law and Order League" routed 250 pickets in a battle near Glenwood, Iowa. Farm protest leader Milo Reno continued to stir up discontent with attacks on Agriculture Secretary Henry Wallace and on the entire Roosevelt administration. Wallace's farm policy "betrayed agriculture," Reno said.

Reno, a onetime Iowa farmer who had been trained for the ministry, was the key man in the national farm protest and president of the national "Farmers Holiday" movement. He cut a distinctive figure, wearing a wide-brimmed hat over a thick mane of hair, sporting a red necktie and horn-rimmed glasses and quoting the Bible in a ringing voice. He insisted that the holiday group was "simply demanding the same consideration for our industry in the same way as other institutions obtain theirs; that is, to refuse to deliver the products of our farms for less than production costs."

The growing army of farmers opposed to Reno wanted him muzzled and the president of a "Law and Order League" at Le Mars demanded that the newspapers give Reno "no more publicity." *The Tribune* took issue with that demand in an editorial that said: "*The Tribune* will not, so long as it remains free to decide its own policies, agree to such censorship. . . . As for Mr. Reno, *The Tribune* disagrees with him in this whole farm strike business. It has said so and will continue to say so. But it does not believe that the correct answer, or the safe answer, or the American answer, is to say in effect to him: 'Nothing that you say will be considered news.' For that is what a demand for ceasing to 'give publicity' comes down to."

The editorial made a free-press, free-speech point that

editors are obliged to make decade after decade, incident after incident, to the reading public. The paper, the editorial said, did not aim to give "publicity" to anyone, but:

"It does aim to print the news — all of it, whether it likes the taste of the current supply or not. It believes that the cause of American civilization, of democracy in the world, of freedom and liberty of every kind is dependent more on full and free and fast ventilation of ideas — in other words on free speech and free press — than anything else in the whole wide world.

"The test of free speech and free press, as long ago was said, is not in allowing to be said the things we like to hear but in allowing to be said the things we find unpleasant."

Editorializing about the northwest Iowa farm picket actions, The Register meanwhile counseled: "Direct action now is especially dangerous, because it sets an ominous example for a country full of unemployed, facing winter, in a period of widespread irritability. Up to now we have been congratulating ourselves on having got through three depression years without noteworthy violence. The use of violence to enforce blockades of Iowa cities, the counter use of force in terms of tear gas and clubs and the psychological mounting of submachine guns on jails in which picketers have been placed, are not the best imaginable assurances of continuance of that record."

When federal farm programs finally started putting money in rural pockets, the farm strikers lost their momentum. In November of 1933, the government began lending corn growers 45 cents a bushel, far above the market, on corn sealed in the farmers' own corncribs. The violent "farm revolution" of the 1930s had come to an end.

Farm problems were not the only subject The Register dealt with emphatically in the early 1930s. The recurring problems of joblessness and racial equality also were editorial topics.

Massive unemployment and a proposal for a five-day week brought a commentary that attempted to convince businessmen of their stake in cutting unemployment.

The Register wrote of the five-day week proposal: "For one thing, it should be realized that this is no visionary program, aimed solely at uplifting the wage-earner. The interests of capital and management are, in the last analysis, as intimately concerned in solution of the unemployment problem as those of the workers themselves...."

The primary object, it should be clear, is not to create more leisure for those now employed, but to create jobs for unemployed workmen. To decry the movement as the 'outgrowth of Bolshevik propaganda,' as one Iowa executive did, is therefore to betray utter misunderstanding. . . . It is industrial capital that has benefited from introduction of machine methods in production. To the extent, therefore, that machines are responsible for the permanent surplus of workers, capital should share in the cost of re-creating jobs to take care of that surplus. Unemployment relief, it is generally conceded today, constitutes an obligation upon society. And it is surely better to give work than to give money in the form of the dole."

On the race issue, discussing "The Problem of the Negro Vote," a Sept. 7, 1932 *Register* editorial addressed itself to the nomination of Negro James W. Ford as the vice-presidential candidate of the Communist party. Six million adult blacks entitled to vote were "not wholly without leadership or mediums of expression," it said. "Anyone who has ever seen the Negro publication, *The Crisis*, edited by the well-known writer W. E. B. DuBois, will understand that the educated Negro is capable of and is attaining intelligent expression of his attitude toward the society in which he lives." Educated blacks, it said, were "perhaps not overenthusiastic about the sudden lurch of Negro support toward the Communist party. But . . . there are only two parties which have taken any pains to curry the favor of the large Negro working class — the Socialists and the Communists — or at least to curry it so that the mass of Negroes take any serious stock in it."

Citing *Crisis*'s emphasis on "a constantly growing proportion of the Negroes . . . demanding the right to become articulate," the editorial said the white majority might just as well plan on blacks making themselves heard eventually. "The Negro," it said, "is learning to . . . comprehend national affairs. He is finding able and honest leaders within his own ranks from among the thousands graduating from colleges and professional schools. He is going to take his rightful part in government, someway."

Toward the end of the Cowles-Ingham era, *The Register* found itself in the center of a nationwide controversy over America's drift toward war. The paper faced another case of separating news coverage from its editorial viewpoint in dealing with a national hero — flier Charles Lindbergh.

The Nazis had overwhelmed most of Western Europe;

only Britain stood in the way of a complete German victory. In July of 1940, *The Register* editorially approved substantial aid to Britain, declaring: "Everything in the world-wide picture ... makes it obvious from America's standpoint it is desirable for Britain to hold." As the war expanded in 1941 and Hitler's armies turned on the Soviet Union, the United States slowly began mobilizing National Guardsmen.

Meanwhile, Lindbergh, on a speaking tour under the auspices of the isolationist America First Committee, came to Des Moines to challenge the relative Iowa coolness to the America Firsters' demand that the United States stay out of the war. The lack of support was attributed largely to the attitudes of *The Register* and *The Tribune* and to Iowa-born Vice-President Henry Wallace.

The Register gave plentiful coverage to the Des Moines meeting in the old Coliseum on the banks of the Des Moines River. The Lindbergh staff later expressed appreciation for the fairness of the news coverage — while calling the papers' editorial position on the international situation 100 per cent wrong. Before the meeting, a *Register* editorial addressed to Lindbergh said: "Since we really believe in freedom and have tried to stand consistently for it, we concede ... your right to have your say — to say it here — to say it without interference as persuasively as you can." But, regarding Lindbergh's contention that the United States should not help Britain, the editorial said to the flier: "We think your main judgments are 'all wet.' "

Lindbergh spoke at the Coliseum Sept. 11, 1941 to 8,000 persons. Immediately before his speech, the crowd heard a piped-in radio broadcast of one of President Roosevelt's "fireside chats," in which F.D.R. startled the country by announcing that he had ordered the U.S. Navy to attack any German or Italian warships in the Atlantic patrol zone without waiting to be fired upon. The Roosevelt speech took the top headlines the next day — despite the fact that Lindbergh had provoked the angriest nationwide reaction of his career in his own speech.

Lindbergh told his cheering, booing, heckling audience that "the three most important groups who have been pressing this country toward war are the British, the Jewish and the Roosevelt administration." What touched off controversy, though, was a further statement regarding the Jews. "Their greatest danger in this country," he said, "lies in their large ownership and influence in our motion pictures, our press, our radio and our government."

Waymack wrote on the editorial page the next day: "Frankly . . . it was the Colonel's worst speech, so intemperate, so unfair, so dangerous in its implications that it can not but turn many spadefuls of dirt in the digging of the grave of his influence in this crisis. . . . It was essentially a 'smear' speech."

Waymack rejected the implication that Jews were any more anti-Hitler or culpable because of it than the general run of Americans and pointed out Lindbergh's failure to attribute the American drift toward war to the German military successes and "the invasions of innocent neutrals and the terrifying collapse of France."

Late in the Cowles-Ingham days the issues to be faced — censorship, bigotry, war, crime, human dignity — were the same as they had been in the early years and as they were to continue to be in later years. Through that hectic decade of the 1930s and into the 1940s, the two founders of Twentieth Century *Register* continued to keep their hands in.

To help Herbert Hoover, Gardner Cowles had gone to Washington, D. C., as a member of the Reconstruction Finance Corporation, on recommendation of President Hoover's good friend, cartoonist Jay Darling. Cowles did not depart from his conservative philosophy while he was at the R.F.C. He wanted "strict security for the government on all loans," an associate said. "He wanted to see the government get its money back. He did not favor 'blue sky' loans. If the management of a corporation proved incompetent, he favored kicking that management out."

With the change in administrations, Gardner Cowles in 1933 gladly returned to Des Moines to stay. At age 72, he was suffering from a long-troublesome eye ailment that had worsened in recent years and caused his sons to question whether he ought to take the R.F.C. post when it was offered. By the mid-1930s, nearly all of his reading had to be done for him by others. Secretary Opal Wilson, for one, read to him on Saturday afternoons at the office. "I read *Time* magazine out loud, cover to cover," she said. "When there wasn't much news in the magazine, he would say: 'Opal, it's getting to be too much mustard and pickles.' "

In the late 1930s, he had some vision left and he came to the office as usual on Sundays and had someone read to him mail that was addressed to him personally. In later years, his hearing also was impaired, which brought him to comment, *a propos* Editor Ingham's lifelong digestive ailment: "With Harvey Ingham's eyes and ears and my stomach, we'd make a good man." He also underwent eye operations and treatment at the Mayo Clinic in Rochester, Minn. — to little avail. Reporter Agnes Arney recalled that he once said in a moment of dejection: "Agnes, why on earth did I lose my eyes? I have been a careful man. I haven't done any dissipating, and here I have lost my eyes."

The last years of his life were not easy for Gardner Cowles. He could not see at all, and could not hear normally. He attended stockholder meetings and sessions of the board of directors. Yet he knew there was a gulf between him and the business he loved so much.

"Father felt he should be at the helm of *The Register* as he had been for so many years," a member of the family said. "He could not stand not being able to see and to know what was going on. He was so cut off from everything."

In those twilight years, however, he still could hear well enough to be read to. Family members and others read to him constantly. He wanted to know the stock market quotations every day and if a reader skipped a quotation, he knew it, because he knew the list by heart — at least the list of the major stocks.

In the winter of 1945-46, Gardner Cowles told one visitor who was leaving on a vacation: "I probably won't be here when you return."

He was correct. He died at 7:15 p.m. Feb. 28, 1946 in his home at 100 Thirty-seventh Street in Des Moines. It was his eighty-fifth birthday anniversary.

A farewell editorial on Gardner Cowles in *The Register,* written by Editor Bill Waymack, said:

"He saw storms rise. He weathered them. He saw Iowa weather them. He saw America weather them. He believed in America. He believed in Iowa. He was an optimist to the end. . . . He sent out many caravans, did that boy of frontier days. They came back laden with different things. They came back with nothing finer than the respect and warm friendship of those who worked with him and under him long."

Editor Emeritus Harvey Ingham died at age 90 on Aug. 21, 1949, near the end describing himself "worn out but still optimistic." One of the finest tributes to him appeared in his own newspaper, which said editorially: "Wherever he was, whatever he did, to whatever controversy he set his pen, with whomsoever he associated, he made men think, and made them think more kindly."

Several years before his death, in a statement on his eighty-fourth birthday, Ingham had summed up the still-consistent views of his twilight years: "I am guarded from a state of mind of terror and despair by a firm belief in the essential goodness of life and in the evolution by some process or other, which I do not know and can not determine, of a higher and nobler humanity."

The success of the teamwork of Gardner Cowles and Harvey Ingham rested ultimately upon a winning combination of pragmatism and idealism. They and *The Des Moines Register* grew up with their country, up and out of that period of easy isolationism before World War I and into the complexities and moral choices of the Twentieth Century. Cowles's fiscal integrity bred a respect for and nurturing of integrity in the editorial sector of the newspaper, in the public interest, as well as on the business side.

The public interest was in Editor Bill Waymack's mind when he shaped *The Register*'s code more than three decades ago. He called that code "The Three Commandments Guiding the *Register* and *Tribune*." They read — as they do on a large plaque in today's Register and Tribune Building:

"1. We believe in presenting all the news impartially and objectively in the news columns.

"2. We believe in expressing our own opinions as persuasively and forcefully as possible, but only on the editorial pages.

"3. We believe in giving our readers the opinions of other competent writers representing all sides of controversial issues in order that our readers may form their own judgments."

Out of that "little and weak" newspaper into which the two Nineteenth Century individualists breathed size and strength grew a Twentieth Century newspaper that continues to bear the imprint of their personalities.

12 THE CONTINUING IMPRINT

The Ingham and Cowles traditions carry on today, long after Harvey Ingham and Gardner Cowles, sr. have died. And today, as in the early part of the century, a Cowles runs the noneditorial side and a non-family-member runs the editorial side.

Today, David Kruidenier, a grandson of Gardner Cowles, sr., is president and publisher of the newspapers. Michael Gartner, who started out answering telephones in the *Register* sports department, now is editor.

Gartner succeeded Kenneth MacDonald as editor in 1976. MacDonald took the title of editorial chairman for one year and then retired at the beginning of 1977, ending 50 years with the papers. MacDonald served the papers longer than Ingham and clearly matched in him in influence both within the corporation and within the state.

Like Ingham, MacDonald provided enlightened leadership. He was calm but unyielding in his goal, and his goal was to insure that the newspapers remain a state-wide voice and the state remain a progressive one.

"Without a literate, alert, progressive community, no newspaper can endure," he said.

The Register did more than endure during his tenure. Under MacDonald, *The Register* and *The Tribune* were among the first general-circulation newspapers to look at such diverse subjects as conservation, education, medicine, ultility regulation, religion and the arts as regular sources of news. Under him, *The Register* became the country's premier daily newspaper in American agriculture and one of the few provincial newspapers whose voice was heard in Washington.

During MacDonald's tenure, first as head of the news department and then as head of the news and editorial pages, many *Register* and *Tribune* staff members won Pulitzer Prizes. Among them was James Risser, a staff member hired and encouraged by MacDonald, who won the Pulitzer the year MacDonald stepped down.

MacDonald ran the papers under a kind of *laissez-faire* system, allowing reporters and writers great latitude in choosing subjects and approaches, so long as the result was fair and literate. The list of Pulitzer Prize winners under MacDonald, his predecessor and his successor illustrates the breadth of interests supported by the policy of MacDonald and *The Register*:

- Jay N. (Ding) Darling, 1924, for his cartoon entitled "In the Good Old U.S.A," which showed how men of humble birth could succeed in the United States through hard work.
- W.W. Waymack, 1938, for editorial writing, based on his full year's output, including editorials on farm problems and civil liberties.
- Forrest W. Seymour, 1943, for editorial writing, based on a full year's output, including a prominent editorial on "Statesmanship in the American Legion."
- Jay Darling, also 1943, his second Pulitzer for cartooning, for a cartoon entitled "What a Place for a Waste Paper Salvage Campaign" which pictured the U.S. Capitol buried under government reports and press releases.
- Nat Finney, 1948, for national reporting, based on his disclosure of administration plans to impose war-style censorship on governmental bureaus.
- John Robinson and Don Ultang, 1952, for news photography. Their sequence of photographs during a Drake University-Oklahoma A & M football game showed Drake star Johnny Bright's jaw being broken by an opponent's punch.
- Richard Wilson, 1954, for national reporting, based on his exclusive publication of the FBI report to the White House in the Harry Dexter White espionage case.
- Lauren Soth, 1956, for editorial writing, based on his editorial inviting the Soviet Union to send a delegation to study Iowa's farming methods.
- Clark Mollenhoff, 1958, for national reporting, based on his exposure of labor-union racketeering.
- Frank Miller, 1963, for cartooning, based on a cartoon illustrating the folly of nuclear war.
- Nick Kotz, 1968, for national reporting, based on his investigations into unsanitary conditions in many meat-packing plants.

● James Risser, 1976, for national reporting, based on his disclosure of corruption and other wrongs in the grain-export business.

That record enabled *The Register* to run eye-catching ads saying: "In the history of journalism, only one newspaper has won more Pulitzer Prizes for national reporting than *The Des Moines Register*. Our congratulations to *The New York Times*."

The Pulitzers were won because MacDonald gave his reporters the time and the freedom to pursue subjects not normally pursued by newspapers. They did not come from the luck of being in the right place at the right time.

"Many prize-winning stories come from leaks, tips or explosive events at which a particular reporter just happened to be present," Michael Gartner wrote in a story giving the background of the prize won by James Risser. "But from the beginning, the grain stories have resulted from old-fashioned, hard-digging reporting — searching through documents, searching out people."

Risser's stories irritated many executives. One corporation executive flew into Des Moines in a private jet, hired a widely known local lawyer and threatened to sue. But the lawyer, who knew *The Register*'s obsession with accuracy, instead persuaded the executive to check into the facts first. The executive did, and he found Risser's allegations to be accurate. He quietly returned home.

"An editor had better be prepared to lose most of his friends, because sooner or later you're going to irritate or aggravate anybody you know," MacDonald said.

And the pressure did not always come from just local friends. John and Mike Cowles were called upon more than once during the presidential administrations of Dwight Eisenhower and Lyndon Johnson to curb the digging, driving style of Washington reporter Clark Mollenhoff. "Mollenhoff is a great investigative reporter," Mike Cowles said, "but he is an abrasive fellow. He got under the skin of President Eisenhower. Clark asked rough questions at press conferences. The President didn't like that.

"Ike's friends used to say to me, 'My God, why do you have a fellow like Mollenhoff working for you in Washington?' And we heard the same thing under Lyndon Johnson."

But Mollenhoff was never muzzled. In fact, neither John nor Mike Cowles ever mentioned presidential pressure to

Mollenhoff. It is notable that pressure from President Johnson was being applied at a time when the Cowleses had a sensitive television-licensing problem pending before the Federal Communications Commision and were vulnerable to government pressure.

Local pressure is sometimes more difficult to deal with, but *The Register* has consistently withstood it. The newspaper regularly has stood fast when advertisers have pulled out their business because of unhappiness with news and editorial pages. *The Register* and *The Tribune*, if they gave in to advertisers' whims, MacDonald would say, would no longer be effective sales mediums because readers would sense they were not getting all the news.

MacDonald, upon his retirement, told a reporter: "I've never had an occasion when Mike Cowles or Dave Kruidenier or any member of the Cowles family insisted that I do something that I didn't think the paper should do."

Kruidenier, who became publisher in 1970, is a man very much like his Uncle Mike Cowles. Both would have made great editors had they not been involved in the business operation. Both are insatiably curious, both instinctively know news and both are fluent writers. Perhaps for those reasons, both have given the editors unparalleled freedom.

After Kruidenier became publisher, the newspapers became even more aggressive in their local coverage. By the mid-1970s, the papers were regularly printing salaries of executives of publicly owned companies, were investigating the power structure and infrastructure in Des Moines and were treating sensitive business news — the bad and the embarrassing as well as the good and the pleasing — as Page One material.

All this caused great consternation in some quarters. Many businessmen believe the papers should be an extension of the Chamber of Commerce and they cannot understand the *Register*'s approach.

"The most difficult thing I've encountered is to get the public to understand what the real function of a newspaper is," MacDonald said in late 1976. "It's extremely difficult to get people to understand and accept the concept that the real function of a newspaper is news coverage and that it isn't to be *for* or *against* anything.

"One of the reasons they fail to understand is that a newspaper is also a business, and it's extremely difficult for many to understand that you can make a decision that isn't strictly a business decision."

One reason *The Register* intensified its coverage of business in the 1970s is because of the arrival of Michael Gartner. Though Gartner began his career at *The Register* (and attended college on a scholarship provided to children of employees), he spent 14 years at *The Wall Street Journal,* where he was Page One editor by the time MacDonald and Kruidenier asked him to return to Des Moines as executive editor in 1974.

While Michael Gartner was covering business with increased emphasis, David Kruidenier was insuring that *The Register* would continue to be a successful business itself.

In the early 1970s, the papers began a multimillion-dollar conversion of the company's printing facilities, replacing Linotype machines and even typewriters with computers. By 1976, the change was complete, and the Des Moines newspapers were among the most modern in the world.

Cost savings in the production process had become mandatory over the years. The papers were built on the premise of cheap newsprint and cheap gasoline (and some would say cheap labor), and as newsprint and gasoline prices vaulted newspapers throughout the country began changing outmoded production processes.

The changes enabled *The Register* to remain a state-wide paper, among the last of that breed in America. And as the new management adopted and adapted the tenets handed down by Gardner Cowles, sr. and Harvey Ingham, the papers and the corporation continued to thrive. The news and editorial side continued to search vigorously for excellence; the marketing, production and business side continued to strive for success.

"If we weren't a successful business," Kenneth MacDonald said upon his retirement, "we couldn't be a responsible newspaper. And I think it's an article of faith that a democratic society can't exist unless it has a competent, responsible form of communication, so that people can understand the type of community they live in."

INDEX

Reno, Milo: 154
Republican Party: 13, 14, 40, 41, 58, 73, 74
Risser, James: Pulitzer Prize, 162, 163
Roberts, George: 15, 16, 17, 21, 26
Robinson, John: Pulitzer Prize, 162
Rommel, Erwin: 110
Roosevelt, Franklin Delano: New Deal programs, 51, 142; 1932 Iowa campaign, 148-49; Supreme Court-packing plan, 124, 144; mentioned, 88, 91, 104, 109, 119, 124, 145, 151, 152, 157
Roosevelt, Mrs. Franklin D.: 96, 119-20
Roosevelt, Theodore: 23, 41-42, 119
Rounds, J. G.: 60
Russell, J Stuart (Jim): 125-26, 142, 147

Sacco, Nicola: 72, 73
Sac County Bulletin: 125
Sacco-Vanzetti case: 72-73
Scopes, John: 75
Selby, Rodney: 69-70, 136
Seymour, Forrest: 55, 56; Pulitzer Prize, 162
Shaw, Leslie: 14
Sherman Anti-Trust Act: 23
Sigma Delta Chi: 101, 121
Sioux City Journal: 114, 115, 122
Smith, James: 15
Smuts, Jan Christian: 92
Soth, Lauren: Pulitzer Prize, 110, 162
Southwell, William B.: 89
Spellman, Francis Cardinal: 93
Spencer, Iowa: 1931 fire, 145
Spirit Lake massacre: 9
Stalin, Josef: 88, 104, 110
Stanton, Elizabeth Cady: 10
Starr, Milton: 8, 9
Stassen, Harold: 100
Steinman, Harold: 129
Strauss, Samuel: 15, 16, 17, 21
Strickland, Maurice: 129
Successful Farming magazine: 74
Sullivan, Mark: 119, 151
"Sunlight on Your Doorstep" (Bradley L. Morison): 96
Supreme Court-packing plan: 124, 144

Taft, Robert A.: 104
Taft, William Howard: 41-42

Tass: Soviet news agency, 111
Taylor, Garner W. (Sec): 127-30
Time magazine: 99, 106, 108, 158
Today magazine: 95
Trigg, Joe: 33
Truman, Harry S: 88, 99, 100, 119
Turner, Dan: 147, 150
Turner, Mrs. Dan: 149, 150

Ultang, Don: Pulitzer Prize, 162
United Nations: 46, 99
The Upper Des Moines (Algona): 4, 8, 11, 14

Vandenberg, Arthur: 104
Vanzetti, Bartolomeo: 72, 73
Venture magazine: 103

Wade, Judge Martin: 22
Wallace, Henry A.: 21, 51, 120, 124, 142, 144, 157
Walters, Basil (Stuffy): 19, 56, 60, 94, 95, 96, 135, 136, 143
Watts, Harry: 57
Waymack, William W. (Bill): 122-24; and farm issues, 122-23; Pulitzer Prize, 123, 162; "Three Commandments" of *Register* and *Tribune*: 160; mentioned, 55, 63, 107, 124, 126, 127, 130, 133, 137, 158, 159
Wayne, Priscilla (Mrs. Wayne Sprague): 68
White, Fred, 66
White, Harry Dexter, 162
Wilchinski, Norman: 80
Wilcots, Henry: 59
Williams, Allie: 36
Willkie, Wendell: 104-10 *passim*
Wilson, Opal: 61, 158
Wilson, Richard: Pulitzer Prize, 145, 162; Washington coverage, 142-45 *passim*
Wilson, Woodrow: 42-46, 55, 58, 91
Women's suffrage: 47, 57
Wood, Leonard: 73
Wright, Bearcat: 129-30

Yates, George: 61, 130-35, 145
Young, Lafayette, jr.: 76-77
Younkers, department store: 76